The Herefordshire School of Romanesque Sculpture

The
Herefordshire School
of Romanesque Sculpture

by

Malcolm Thurlby

Logaston Press

LOGASTON PRESS
Little Logaston Woonton Almeley
Herefordshire HR3 6QH
logastonpress.co.uk

First published by Logaston Press 1999
Reprinted 2000, 2002, 2005, 2006, 2008
Copyright © Malcolm Thurlby 2008

ISBN 978 1873827 60 4

Set in Times by Logaston Press
and printed in Great Britain by
Biddles Ltd., King's Lynn

To Carol

Contents

ACKNOWLEDGMENTS

George Zarnecki has nurtured my interest in Romanesque sculpture ever since our first meeting some thirty years ago. Many friends and colleagues have discussed aspects of the Herefordshire School with me. I should like to thank Ron Baxter, Eileen Robertson Hamer, Stuart Harrison, Martin Henig, Sandy Heslop, Larry Hoey, Jim King, Kathleen Lane, Peter Lasko, Richard Morris (University of Warwick), David Robinson, Roger Stalley and in particular Eric Fernie who kindly read a draft of the text. My students at York University, Ontario, have been a constant inspiration, especially Ewa Chwojko, Peter Coffman, Jean Gardiner, Karen Lundgren and Hugh McCague. Paul Williamson, keeper of sculpture at the Victoria and Albert Museum, arranged a private viewing of the Deposition ivory and the Gloucester Candlestick. The photograph of the Deposition ivory is also reproduced courtesy of the Victoria and Albert Museum. Anna Eavis of the Royal Commission on Historical Monuments supplied photographs of the plaster casts of the Shobdon arches. Mrs V. McSorley graciously gave access to the Bell Inn at Alveley, Shropshire. Thanks are also due to Hereford Cathedral Library for use of the transparency of f.3 on MS P.IV.3 used on the rear cover, and to Brian Byron for drawing the location map.

Last but by no means least, thanks are due to Andy Johnson and Ron Shoesmith for sound editorial advice.

PREFACE

At school in England it had been my intention to concentrate on the sciences—chemistry in particular held a great appeal. That was until 'O-level' year when one of my extra subjects was art, the curriculum for which included a paper on the history of architecture in England. One of the recommended books was J. Charles Cox and Charles Bradley Ford, *The Parish Churches of England*, in which plate 55 detailed the south doorway of Kilpeck church. The appeal of that image was instant. At that very moment I knew my life had changed—chemistry had been eclipsed by Romanesque sculpture. The love affair continues and the passion I feel for Kilpeck grows stronger with each visit. My father, Lionel Thurlby, indulged this passion. Before I was old enough to drive he chauffeured me from our home in Rickmansworth, Hertfordshire, to Kilpeck and other Romanesque churches in Herefordshire and throughout the country. On those trips we were accompanied by Godfrey Cornwall, local historian of Rickmansworth, who instilled in me the importance of taking good photographs for art-historical investigation. The lesson seems all the more profound at a time when historiography (the history of the discipline) is often seen as an end in itself rather than a prelude to a thorough investigation of the work of art in the context for which it was created, and when theoretical considerations become so all-consuming that some even dispense with the image! Let us not forget that we are dealing with works of art which are intended to have a visual impact. Therefore, the reader is here presented with the most complete set of photographs of the sculptures of the Herefordshire School published to date. Many are illustrated for the first time, including a large number of the corbels of Kilpeck church. The illustrations are made from original Kodachrome slides taken on Canon equipment with 20mm to 500mm, and 24mm and 35mm perspective-control, lenses.

Endnotes are included in preference to parenthetic references or footnotes. Full references are given in the bibliography.

Map showing the location of buildings mentioned in and adjoining Herefordshire in the text

INTRODUCTION

In studies of the many regional manifestations of twelfth-century sculpture in Britain, the greatest attention has been devoted to the Herefordshire School. Quite apart from the obvious aesthetic appeal of the lavish decoration of Kilpeck church or the fonts of Castle Frome and Eardisley, the Herefordshire School has fascinated art historians because of the diversity of its sources. Connections are made abroad with Santiago de Compostella, western France, Ireland, Scandinavia and Italy, and in England with the Celtic tradition, Anglo-Saxon art, with the sculpture of Reading Abbey, Tewkesbury Abbey, Hereford Cathedral, St Peter's Abbey (now cathedral) at Gloucester, with the so-called Bromyard or Dymock school of sculpture, and with work commissioned by Bishop Roger for Old Sarum Cathedral (1102-39). Parallels have been cited in different media—metalwork, ivory carving, wood sculpture and manuscript illumination. In view of this seemingly exhaustive investigation one might think that there would be little more to say on the subject, and why this book?

The answer is threefold. First, for the most part the sculpture has been studied in isolation from the building of which it formed an integral part. It is here proposed to see the sculpture in its architectural context. This involves the examination of richly decorated churches, like Kilpeck, alongside less ornate ones of similar plan, like Moccas and Peterchurch. Secondly, scholarship on the Herefordshire School has focussed on the style of the sculpture. The fundamental contribution in this area was made by Jerzy (George) Zarnecki.[1] He identified two leading sculptors in the school whom he designated the Chief Master and the Aston Master, the latter so-called because Zarnecki suggested that he first worked on the tympanum of the north doorway of St Giles at Aston. The Aston Master moved to Shobdon where he collaborated with the Chief Master. Both sculptors then worked at Kilpeck and subsequently executed a number of other works of the school. I think that this basic identification of the sculptors holds true and will form an essential part of this study. Art-historical scholarship now places great emphasis on avenues of investigation other than style analysis. Michael Clanchy observed that 'Country churches were not as remote from cosmopolitan culture as they appear today. They were built by well-travelled lords who were their patrons, rather than by a parish community. The richness of the Herefordshire School of stone carving ... is best explained in this way.'[2] In a review of the exhibition of English Romanesque art held at the Hayward Gallery, London, in 1984, Ian Wood suggested that great issues, like the impact of the Conquest, 'should be explored in specific terms by tracing the influence of particular patrons and associations.'[3] A similar sentiment was expressed by Jeffrey West who advocated a patron-based approach to the study of Romanesque sculpture.[4] The challenge was taken up by Eileen Robertson Hamer in her Ph.D dissertation for the University of Chicago. Hamer examined the Herefordshire School in connection with the 'development of Norman lordship and evolution of parish churches along the Welsh border ... [in order] to see the churches in context and come to some understanding of their meanings for those who commissioned, built and used them.'[5] Hamer made an important contribution and I hope that she will soon publish her work. The aim of this book is to see the sculpture of the Herefordshire School in the context for which it was created and is similar to Hamer's and owes much to her pioneering study. My approach involves the integration of 'new' and traditional art history; on the one hand, the role of the patron in determining the form of the church and the extent and meaning of the sculptural programme, on the other, matters of style and technique provide the key to understanding something about the artists who created the work.

And so to the third, and perhaps the major, reason for the book. Hamer's dissertation is unpublished and Zarnecki's thesis only briefly summarized in his 1953 book, long since out of print. Most of the remaining discussion on the Herefordshire School has appeared in academic journals which are difficult to obtain for those without access to university libraries. This book, therefore, aims at that delicate balance between appeal to the scholar and to the general public. It must be confessed that this is a somewhat daunting task. On the one hand, the art historian approaches the text with prior knowledge of the specialized literature and will seek insights into the minutiae of the subject and new perspectives on the historical setting of the work. On the other hand, there is the reader with no prior knowledge of the topic, a person, like me thirty years ago, who is captivated by the aesthetic experience of the south doorway of Kilpeck church. Both the professional art historian and the non-specialist will have a set of questions. Those of the non-specialist are likely to be more general but at the same time may be more profound, unencumbered as they are by the weight of previous art-historical investigation or coloured by current trends in the discipline. When and why was it built/carved? By whom? What does it mean? How long did it take to carve/build? Where did they learn to carve like that? What tools did they use? How much did it cost? These questions are not easily answered. Even where documentation exists, it is only in the case of Shobdon that there is reference to the construction of the church and the name of the patron — and here the document is only dated within the 12-year period 1131-43. Elsewhere, Kilpeck church was given to St Peter's Abbey, Gloucester, in 1134, and it is likely that it was completed by that date. Hereford Cathedral is dated 1107/15-1142/8. Leominster Priory was refounded by King Henry I in 1123 as a daughter house of Reading Abbey. For the other works the sculpture is accompanied in most cases by the architectural setting and surroundings. For these the patron is not specifically mentioned and therefore deductions are made from references to ownership of the land in the Domesday Survey (1087) and from records of the gifts of churches in monastic charters. While documentation on the patrons and dating is thin, for the sculptors it is non-existent. The work of art alone is the document. Specific motifs, technique and style provide the clues as to where the sculptors might have been trained. Was the architect/master mason the same person as the master sculptor? Are there suggestions that the sculptors were involved with the production of the sumptuous arts of manuscript illumination, metalwork or ivory carving? Is it possible to infer anything about their status in society? Answers to these questions can only attempted after careful examination of the works themselves and by analogy with documented cases elsewhere.

The organization of the material has not been an easy matter. In view of the lack of precise dates a hypothetical chronological path did not seem realistic. Particular motifs might have been chosen as salient features in order to demonstrate uniformity within the various examples of the school. While this would have the advantage of clearly establishing the existence of the Herefordshire School, it has the disadvantage of jumping from one site to another without ever coming to understand the sculpture of a building as a whole and setting it in its context. Therefore, it has been decided to deal with each site separately. The book commences with a brief historical background to both the Romanesque and the pre and post-Conquest background to the region, leading to an introduction to the major patrons of the school. The sources of inspiration and examples which might have been followed are then discussed, with specific reference to the work at Kilpeck, the prime surviving example of the work of the Herefordshire School. This is followed by a brief consideration of the role and status of the master craftsmen, and of their training and background.

These chapters then set the scene for the detailed investigation of the individual works of the Herefordshire School. This begins with Kilpeck, the best-known, best-preserved and the richest extant example of the school. From there proceed to Shobdon, which was originally even richer than Kilpeck, but now, alas, is but a shadow of its former glory. Shobdon Church was pulled down in the mid-18th century and its two doorways and chancel arch were re-erected as a folly, 'improved' with Gothick gables. Today they stand badly eroded[6], but fortunately stabilized in a recent restoration. Our appreciation and understanding of the Shobdon arches is enhanced by the publication of Lewis's lithographs in 1852 and by photographs of 19th-century casts of the arches—the casts themselves (with the exception of the Ascension/Christ in Majesty tympanum which is today preserved in the Victoria and Albert Museum) perished in the fire which destroyed the Crystal Palace in 1936. The other works of the school are arranged, where possible, according to patron or family connection. Each work is described and related to other works of the school previously discussed. Where applicable other influences on the sculpture are investigated and the meaning of the sculpture and the church as a whole is interpreted.

CHAPTER 1

The Historical Background

The Herefordshire School of sculpture is a product of the patronage of the Norman rulers of the Welsh Marches in the second quarter of the twelfth century. As such it may be called 'Norman' and in the context of European art of the period it is 'Romanesque'. Romanesque is an international style with manifestations throughout Europe from the late eleventh to the late twelfth century, although the duration varied from one region to another. The label 'Romanesque' is a good one, for there are often precise analogues with regional Roman works, something most readily appreciated today in Provence where the relatively high rate of preservation of Roman and Romanesque buildings facilitates direct comparison between 'model' and 'copy'. The large scale of the most ambitious Romanesque churches follows metropolitan Roman models, both ecclesiastical and secular—the vast German imperial cathedral of Speyer, commenced about 1030, recalls two great fourth-century edifices of the Emperor Constantine: the cathedral of Old St Peter's in Rome and the Basilica in Trier. In the same tradition, the high vaults added throughout Speyer Cathedral in the late eleventh century recreate the great masonry vaults of Roman bath architecture and the Basilica of Maxentius in Rome. In Capetian France the same ambitious scale was adopted for the church of St Remi at Reims (1007-49) and Orléans Cathedral (1030). The technology, articulation and awe-inspiring monumentality of Romanesque buildings depend on Roman precedent.

Similarly, the integration of monumental sculpture in the buildings—the creation of a truly architectural sculpture—is another aspect of the Romanesque revival of Rome. Walls in the largest churches range between six and eight feet in thickness and are constructed with a mortared rubble core faced with ashlar (squared stone). There is a preference for round-headed arches which often have two or three separate steps or orders. These divisions usually correspond with the supports—jambs in a doorway, piers in an arcade. Individual orders of the

1

arches may be left plain or be carved with mouldings which range from simple rolls and hollows to elaborate ornament such as various types of chevron (zigzag). The simplest supports have unornamented, squared orders with a projecting chamfered or moulded impost at the top from which the arch springs. More complex supports juxtapose squared and columnar elements and are topped with carved capitals as in many examples of the Herefordshire School.

In England the revival of building on a large scale commenced around 1050 with Edward the Confessor's Westminster Abbey.[1] In the *Gesta Regum*, the famous historian, William of Malmesbury, observed (*c*.1125) that the Confessor's church was built 'in that style which now all seek to emulate at vast expense.'[2] With the Norman Conquest the rivalry amongst patrons of churches was to intensify.

Following the Conquest, King William appointed William fitz Osbern as earl of Hereford.[3] Fitz Osbern established castles at Wigmore, Clifford and Monmouth, rebuilt those at Hereford and Ewyas Harold, and it is generally assumed that the keep that survives at Chepstow was built by him. Fitz Osbern also founded a priory at Chepstow, the nave of which still stands, albeit without its aisles and high vault.[4] With the establishment of castle and priory he addressed the two basic concerns of the new rulers: secular domination in the form of the castle, and religious leadership and insurance for the afterlife with the church. In so doing he created monumental symbols of Norman authority and culture. In the buildings incorporating the Herefordshire School there is a similar pattern—the foundation and/or generous endowment of a monastery, and/or the construction of a church and castle together and the subsequent presentation of the church to a monastery.

On William fitz Osbern's death in battle in Flanders in 1071, his younger son, Roger de Breteuil, inherited his earldom and English estates. Roger's failed rebellion against the king in 1075 resulted in his imprisonment and forfeiture of his estates. His lands were divided between the Lacy[5] and Mortimer[6] families who thereby became major landowners in Herefordshire. Both families were to become intimately connected with the Herefordshire School.

With the establishment of firm Norman control, massive new church construction was put in hand as patrons sought to outdo each other. William of Malmesbury records that Bishop Maurice of London's (1085-1107) big ideas 'led him to commence but by no means complete a magnificent new church of St Paul (with a spacious crypt) whose size and decoration bad fair to excel those of all others.'[7] With the loss of Old St Paul's this sense of rivalry between patrons is now best appreciated in the great churches which formerly housed relics of major saints as at St Albans Abbey (1077),[8] Winchester Cathedral (1079)[9], Ely Cathedral (1081),[10] Bury St Edmunds Abbey (1081) and Durham

Cathedral (1093).[11] The vast scale of these churches emulates the Constantinian shrine-church of Old St Peter's in Rome, while the spiral columns in the presbytery and transept, and the ribs in the vaults at Durham Cathedral invite the association of the local saint, Cuthbert, with St Peter, inspired as they were by the early christian *baldacchino* above St Peter's shrine. At St Albans Abbey, Winchester Cathedral and Durham Cathedral eastern towers, which originally flanked the main apse, may also reflect Old St Peter's. The external wall passage in the crossing tower at St Albans Abbey is paralleled in San Nazaro in Milan and Speyer Cathedral. The aisled transepts at Winchester Cathedral recall the Pilgrimage Churches such as St Sernin at Toulouse, Orléans Cathedral and St-Remi at Reims, while the eclectic design aims to incorporate 'into one huge scheme all the most elaborate features of the new High Romanesque architecture of Europe.'[12] The same can be said of Durham Cathedral where a new standard was established for lavish arch mouldings.

But the new style of building and the quest for exotic associations was not confined to the largest churches. William of Malmesbury records in the *Gesta Pontificum* that 'Not long after Robert of Lorraine [1079-95] received the see [of Hereford], he built there a church of elegant form, having copied for its design the basilica of Aachen.'[13] This Bishop's Chapel was demolished, with the exception of the north wall, about 1737, but its appearance may be accurately reconstructed with reference to the drawings of William Stukeley, a plan and west elevation commissioned by the Society of Antiquaries, and a vignette of the exterior from the south-west on Taylor's 1757 map of Hereford.[14] While the connection with the Emperor Charlemagne's chapel at Aachen specified by William of Malmesbury has been challenged,[15] not least because of the difficulty of comparing the polygonal plan of the 'model' with the square plan of the 'copy', it is worth remembering that the early ninth-century oratory of Germigny-des-Pres, Loiret, is similar to the Hereford chapel in its square plan with nine bays and a central lantern, and was recorded as a copy of Aachen by a tenth-century commentator. The Aachen and Hereford chapels share an octagonal central lantern, a square, one-bay sanctuary of two storeys, and a huge central entrance arch flanked by spiral staircases leading up to a western tribune. There are also close formal comparisons for the square, nine-bay plans of two-storeys in the palace chapel at Goslar built by Conrad II, *c*.1034-38, in the chapel of Saints Martin and Emmeram at Speyer Cathedral, *c*.1080-90, and in St Godehard's chapel at Mainz Cathedral.[16] This provides an imperial association to the design which may even be extended to the Bodrum Camii in Constantinople, *c*.920.[17] The Bishop's Chapel has no direct bearing on the Herefordshire School of Sculpture but it is significant in that it establishes something exotic and precocious in the region.

Work on replacing the former Anglo-Saxon cathedral at Hereford was commenced by Bishop Reynhelm (1107-15).[18] In both general and specific terms Reynhelm's cathedral continued traditions established in Robert of Lorraine's chapel. There was an imperial connection in the former twin eastern towers.[19] More specifically, the cavernous, multi-ordered portal of the former Romanesque west front of the cathedral (fig.A) was clearly based on this feature in the Bishop's Chapel (fig.B).[20] However, the richly carved decoration of the cathedral doorway contrasted sharply with the plain orders of the Bishop's Chapel portal. It is this aspect of decoration that is so important in the cathedral. From the first there are sculptured capitals, richly moulded arches, and the chip-carved tympana of the presbytery galleries. While the majority of the present detail is the product of the Cottinghams' restoration of the 1840s, the documentation suggests that the new work copied the old wherever

possible.[21] This reading is borne out by comparison of the original capitals of the east presbytery arch and their replacements, and by the capitals remaining in the Vicars' cloister with the crossing capitals and others which were replaced in the church. As will be shown, much of this work, and other architectural elements in the cathedral, provide an important background for the Hereford-shire School.

William of Malmesbury writes of churches springing up after the Conquest in every town and village 'built after a style unknown before.'[22] This copying of the large church in the smaller ones is important to our understanding of the Herefordshire School, for it will be shown that the School's ambitious patrons aimed at nothing less than the emulation of the buildings of the most

Fig.A The former Romanesque west front of Hereford Cathedral

munificent patrons of the day. Their goal was to create small-scale equivalents of the lavish decoration of King Henry I's Reading Abbey or Bishop Roger's Sarum Cathedral. Their works would be just as eclectic as the great churches and, like them, would reflect international sources, regional traditions and the prestigious art of the metalworker.

Work had started on these smaller churches in Herefordshire when, in 1084, Walter de Lacy founded one collegiate church in Hereford, St Peter, and endowed another, St Guthlac, in the castle.[23] In 1101 Walter's son, Hugh, gave the church of St Peter to St

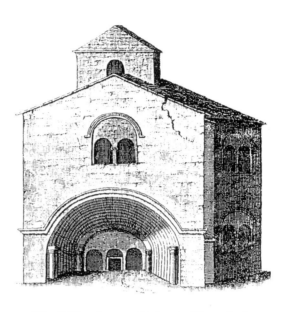

Fig.B The former Bishop's Chapel of Hereford Cathedral with its cavernous doorway

Peter's Abbey (now cathedral) Gloucester at which time Benedictine monks were installed. In 1108 Hugh founded the Augustinian priory of Llanthony.[24] On Hugh's death (1115/21) his lands passed in large part to Payn fitz John through marriage to Sybil de Lacy.[25] Fitz John was a magnate in the diocese of Llandaff by 1119.[26] He is described by Walter Map as the king's chamberlain[27], and was probably sheriff of Shropshire in 1130.[28] Giraldus Cambrensis calls him Lord of Ewyas[29], and it was on his land at Ewyas that he and Sybil de Lacy probably built Rowlstone Church. It will be argued that he was responsible for the construction of a stone castle at Longtown (Ewyas Lacy), and that he and/or Sybil ordered the Castle Frome font.

Payn fitz John was closely associated with Miles of Gloucester, constable to Henry I (1130-36), and sheriff of Gloucestershire and Staffordshire.[30] In 1121 Henry I gave Sybil, daughter of Bernard of Neufmarché, to Miles of Gloucester, and stated that Bernard's estates would pass to Sybil's new husband.[31] Bernard of Neufmarché was Lord of Brecon and founder of Brecon Priory. Miles of Gloucester and Payn fitz John were wealthy and powerful men and the bond between their families was established with the marriage before 1137 of Payn's daughter, Cecily, and Miles' son, Roger.[32] Miles and Payn were responsible for the appointment of Robert de Bethune, prior of Llanthony, as

Bishop of Hereford in 1131,[33] and in 1141 Miles was created Earl of Hereford. The *Gesta Stephani* records that in 'King Henry's time they had raised their power to such a pitch that from the river Severn to the sea, all along the border between England and Wales, they involved everyone in litigation and pressed them with forced services.'[34] In light of such unfavourable character references it is with an implied sense of justice that the account continues: 'But on his [King Henry's] death as they waited, restrained rather by fear of King Stephen than by weakness, for a chance of stirring up rebellion, they both perished in a pitiful way without profit from repentance; Payn, while pursuing the Welsh, was the only man of his company to be killed, shot through the head by a javelin (1137), and Miles, after bringing many troubles on king and kingdom by counsel and deed ... had his breast pierced with a comrade's arrow while hunting deer and died immediately (1143).' He was succeeded as Earl of Hereford by his son, Roger.

Payn fitz John appeared as witness to royal writs from 1115/16.[35] Here he was in the company of Henry of Blois, Bishop of Winchester,[36] Roger, Bishop of Salisbury,[37] and Alexander, Bishop of Lincoln.[38] These bishops, in addition to the king, were the leading patrons of architecture and sculpture, and, like the Herefordshire School patrons, were involved with castle building as well as lavishly decorated churches. A royal link for the patronage of the Herefordshire School is also established through Hugh of Kilpeck, royal forester and patron of Kilpeck Church and Castle.

Ralph de Baskerville held Eardisley and Stretton Sugwas from the Lacys and is most probably the patron of the Herefordshire School sculpture in the churches there. Henry I's charter to St Peter's Gloucester includes Hugh de Lacy and Ralph de Baskerville as witnesses.[39] Between 1147 and 1150 Ralph de Baskerville witnessed with Hugh Forester, amongst others, a treaty between William, Earl of Gloucester, and Roger, Earl of Hereford.[40] Ralph de Baskerville and Hugh Forester both witness Earl Roger's charter to Brecon Priory along with Oliver de Brunesope (Brinsop) and Baderon of Monmouth.[41] The latter is William (II) fitz Baderon, son of the William fitz Baderon who held Monmouth for the king where he built a castle and founded a priory. William (II) fitz Baderon was probably the patron of the Herefordshire School sculpture at Monmouth Priory and Ruardean, Gloucestershire as well as responsible for the decorative stonework in the keep at Goodrich Castle. It will be suggested that Oliver de Brunesope and Oliver de Merlimond, the documented founder of Shobdon church, were one and the same. The *Wigmore Chronicle* records that Lord Hugh Mortimer of Wigmore made Oliver de Merlimond 'chief steward of all his land and manager of all his property.'[42] In this role he was probably responsible for the Herefordshire School work on Mortimer property at Aston,

Herefordshire, Rock and Ribbesford, Worcestershire, and at Alveley, Shropshire, the latter a prebend of the college of St Mary Magdalene at Bridgnorth, after Hugh Mortimer took control of Bridgnorth Castle between 1138 and 1140.[43] It will be suggested that Oliver de Merlimond built the church at Brinsop after his break with Hugh Mortimer in 1143. Indeed, it may well be that Hugh Mortimer's patronage simply took the form of financial backing for the works and that it was Oliver de Merlimond who was responsible for their execution. Oliver was a learned man who was entrusted with the eduction of Hugh Mortimer's son, and was closely associated with Robert de Bethune, Bishop of Hereford (1131-48), one of the leading intellectuals of the region, who had studied under William of Champeaux at the abbey of St Victor in Paris, and with William's former master, Anselm of Laon.[44]

Many of the patrons of the Herefordshire School therefore knew each other and also had contact with the king and the leading architectural patrons of the day. This suggests the existence of an intellectual ambience from which the architecture and sculpture derived its source and meaning.

The relative richness of the decoration in the churches of the Herefordshire School would have been determined by the patron as he paid for the work. The involvement of the patron in church building is nowhere documented, excepting that Walter de Lacy is recorded as having fallen from St Peter's Church in Hereford in 1085 whilst superintending its building, a fall from which he subsequently died.[45] This suggests a hands-on approach, although the degree to which it was the exception or the rule is difficult to determine.

The precise nature of Hugh's role in the detailed design at Kilpeck is hard to ascertain. As financier Hugh must have determined the scale of the church and the general extent of the decoration. He would have been responsible for the inclusion of the rib-vaulted apse, the richly sculpted chancel arch and south doorway, and the carved corbel table. He, or an ecclesiastical adviser, would probably have worked out the themes, although the degree to which he/they dictated the details can not be established. Hugh may have insisted on the inclusion of the knights on the left shaft of the south doorway, and elements like the *Agnus Dei* above the south doorway and on the axis of the apse, the angel and the phoenix on the south doorway, and other key elements, but much of the detail was surely left to the sculptor.

The inclusion of motifs derived from western France in the sculpture at Shobdon and Brinsop, especially the radiating voussoirs, suggests that Oliver de Merlimond, who is known to have been on pilgrimage to Santiago de Campostella returning, in all probability, via western France, was closely involved with the creative process. The iconography of the Ascension/Christ in

Majesty tympana at Shobdon, St Giles Hospital at Hereford, and Rowlstone, the Virgin and Child/Trinity on the Fownhope tympanum, and the Harrowing of Hell/Trinity on the Eardisley font, suggest the intellectual role of the patron or at least of an advisor on the matter. References to the *Bestiary*, the Book of Beasts, at Kilpeck, Shobdon, Rock, Ribbesford and Castle Frome are more difficult to determine in that they range from the precise representation of the ibex at Kilpeck to the more generalized depiction of birds and fish which may indicate a more formal than strictly iconographical connection with the *Bestiary*. This theme is developed in the next chapter.

The diversity of sources in the sculpture of the Herefordshire School and what might be described as a taste for the exotic, in fact conform to the highest standards established by the leading patrons of the of the great churches of post-Conquest England, and continued in even more lavish fashion in the works commissioned by Bishop Roger of Salisbury, King Henry at Reading Abbey, possibly Henry of Blois at Glastonbury Abbey, and Bishop Alexander at Lincoln.

Reflections of the past with Germanic animal ornament and interlace of the early middle ages may be nothing more than the equivalent of the current love of antiques. On the other hand, it may have been a carefully calculated and self-conscious assimilation of indigenous elements into the new Norman works. William the Conqueror did not consider that he usurped the throne, rather that he was the legitimate heir to Edward the Confessor. In this light a policy of integration of the local traditions in the works commissioned by the new Norman lords would make good sense. The new rulers would thereby offer the best of both worlds; they would not just replace, but actually make things better. The ambition to create the best building in Christendom seems to have been the aim for many of the Norman patrons as, for example, in the great churches at St Albans, Winchester and Durham. In each case the design was very eclectic and incorporated elements from a wide range of sources as if to announce the international good taste of the worldly patron. To be associated with this way of thinking seems to have been the aim of the patrons of the Herefordshire School of sculpture. Their work could not compete with the vast scale of the grandest works in Norman Britain but the lavish sculpture gave their churches a regal air. Connections with sculpture in western France, Santiago de Compostella and possibly northern Italy announced a cosmopolitan quality, and the inclusion of motifs from metalwork and sumptuous arts provided an immediate association with the finest church treasures.

CHAPTER 2

Sources, Inspiration and Models

The best known example of the Herefordshire School is Kilpeck, known for the exceptional sculpture lavished on the south doorway, the chancel arch, the west window, together with dragons' heads projecting on the west wall and south-east angle of the nave, a carved corbel table round the entire church, and masks on the boss of the apse vault.

Interpretation of the sculpture at Kilpeck has run the gamut from Lewis' attempt of 1842 'to breathe into Ecclesiastical design the profitable breath of communicative intelligence' — or put more simply to read specific meaning into every detail — to Cust's dismissal of any iconographic interpretation as he felt the sculpture was simply intended for decoration. Cust's 1917 viewpoint was largely upheld by Pevsner,[1] for whom 'the corbels are the best preparation for the profusion of decorative sculpture and fantasy throughout the church', whilst Boase could not hope 'to emulate George Lewis', but neither could he accept 'the view, sometimes put forward, that these intricate but whimsical designs are the mere doodling of the cloistered subconscious.'[2] Current scholarship would favour Boase's view.

When St Bernard of Clairvaux (1091-1153) wrote on cloister sculpture to William, Abbot of St. Thierry, he asked 'what profit is there in those ridiculous monsters, in that marvellous and deformed comeliness, that comely deformity? To what purpose are those unclean apes, those fierce lions, those monstrous centaurs, those half-men, those striped tigers, those fighting knights, those hunters winding their horns? Many bodies are there seen under one head, or again, many heads to a single body. Here is a four-footed beast with a serpent's tail; there a fish with a beast's head. Here again the forepart of a horse trails half a goat behind it, or a horned beast bears the hind quarters of a horse. In short, so many and so marvellous are the varieties of divers shapes on every hand, that we are more tempted to read in the marble than in our books, and to spend the whole day in wondering at these things rather than in meditating the law of God. For God's sake, if men are not ashamed of these follies, why at least do they not shrink from the expense?'

The fact that Bernard describes a considerable variety of creatures suggests his contemporaries were doing just what he despaired—searching for meaning, sometimes multiple or even conflicting meaning. Just as the Bible required interpretation, not least when different passages suggested alternative, even opposite, points of view, so the sculpture on churches, or illuminations in manuscripts, invited meditative reading.[3]

Understanding of the Kilpeck sculpture is greatly enhanced by the *Bestiary*, the Book of Beasts. Derived from the Greek *Physiologus*, which was translated into Latin as early as the fifth century, and which incorporated material from Isidore of Seville's *Etymologiae*, the *Bestiary* described the nature and/or habits of each creature, real or mythical. It reflected on the world of mankind in the realm of nature and so incorporated a moral message for the reader.[4] The earliest extant *Bestiary* manuscript dates from *c*.1120,[5] and the book became extremely popular in the late twelfth century. Connections between English Romanesque sculpture and the *Bestiary* have long been established.

The connection between the *Bestiary* and the Kilpeck sculpture is also not without its problems. It is possible that Hugh of Kilpeck had a personal copy. Admittedly lay ownership would seem to be unusual, but it may be significant that the one documented case of lay use—in the thirteenth-century copy at Oxford[6]—has been fixed to a group of barons of national or international importance based in the Welsh Marches.[7] Could this reflect a tradition of the lay ownership of *Bestiary* manuscripts in the region dating back to the twelfth century? Alternatively, the book may have been available in the cathedral or monastic library at Hereford or Gloucester. If that was the case, did Hugh or one of his associates make the references, or was this within the expertise of the sculptor?

Reference to the *Bestiary* offers a plausible explanation for the appearance of the animals and beasts at Kilpeck, and in the case of the ibex (fig.81) the only possible source. However, not all the Kilpeck beasts appear in the earliest manuscripts of the *Bestiary*. This suggests that a more complete set of references was in circulation before the later years of the twelfth century when the popularity of the book was at its peak.

But clearly the carvers could not have gone ahead with such designs unless the patron of the church had at least concurred with, if not authorised, such work, for if the work causes some astonishment now, it may have caused even more when first executed. Sir Thomas Kendrick contrasts the 'beautiful south door at Kilpeck' on which the decoration was applied 'with only the dimmest

Fig.1 (top) The presbytery of Hereford Cathedral and Fig.2 (bottom) The apse of Kilpeck Church where numerous architectural ornaments have parallels

appreciation of architectural propriety', with the 'majestic' west portals of Lincoln Cathedral and refers to the former as 'simply a provincial Anglo-Norman style, and the unrestrained slap-dash use of copious ornament is sufficiently explained by the word "provincial". That is to say, Kilpeck represents not ... an inherited Saxon or Celtic taste, but a local post-Conquest taste expressed at some distance from the main currents of contemporary fashion.'[8]

While Kilpeck may be geographically far removed from London and is therefore, by definition, 'provincial', it was certainly not removed from the then current fashion in architecture. Indeed, it is just the opposite for it is absolutely up-to-date. The use of a wide range of source material at Kilpeck conforms to the highly eclectic approach which marked the degree of patronage in the great churches after the Conquest, local examples being Hereford Cathedral and the adjoining Robert de Losinga's chapel (1079-95). To a certain extent the taste for rich sculpture at Kilpeck can be explained by the work at Hereford Cathedral, which was still in building at the time Kilpeck was constructed, though, as mentioned in the previous chapter, the sculpture in the cathedral's nave largely takes the form of architectural ornamentations such as chevrons, while at Kilpeck much of the work is figurative. This puts Kilpeck alongside the lavish sculpture at Sarum Cathedral, executed for Bishop Roger of Salisbury, and Reading Abbey, where the patron was King Henry I.

Fig.3 (left) Capitals on presbytery arch at Hereford Cathedral and
Fig.4 (right) Vault capital in apse of Kilpeck Church

Fig.5 (top) The tympanum over the south doorway at Kilpeck. Fig.6 (below) Original crossing capital from Hereford Cathedral. The combination of beaded and striated stems in the foliage on the Kilpeck tympanum repeats that the crossing capital

Clearly this lavish, eclectic approach was seen as a mark of high status appropriate to the lord of Kilpeck, an approach which is especially noticeable when compared with the plainer Romanesque apsidal churches at Moccas and Peterchurch built by the same masons. The rib vault in the apse at Kilpeck is paralleled only in the most ambitious churches of the day and ultimately suggests association with the shrine of St Peter in Rome. Similarly, carved corbel tables were only used in the grandest churches, like Winchester, Ely and Sarum Cathedrals and Reading Abbey. Otherwise in the west country school they only appear at Pershore Abbey.[9] Whether or not an association with the shrine of St James at Santiago de Compostella was intended, through the superposed chancel arch figures at Kilpeck, is difficult to decide, but there can be little doubt that Hugh of Kilpeck intended to create a shrine-like church which had the richness of a precious metal reliquary.

The Influence of Hereford Cathedral

As the centre of the diocese and the geographical centre of the shire, fashions in carving and style at Hereford Cathedral must have exerted a wide influence throughout the area. However, much of the detail now present at the cathedral dates from the time of the Cottinghams' restoration between 1842 and 1850.[10] Nevertheless, the loose fragments of original work now in the corridor to the Vicars' cloister, the capitals from the presbytery's east arch, (now set up by that arch), and other capitals from the presbytery, crossing and nave, can all

Fig.7 (top) Dragon's head at the south-west angle of the nave at Kilpeck Church; Fig.8 (below) Capital from the nave arcade at Hereford Cathedral. The three-strand stems with binding straps on the panel behind the dragon's head are allied to work on the cathedral's capital.

be exactly located by their copies in the cathedral. This suggests that Cottingham did not invent new forms but just reproduced what he found, indicating wide use of Romanesque architectural ornamentation in the cathedral.

Numerous architectural ornaments at Kilpeck are paralleled at Hereford Cathedral. They include the beak-spur bases, saltire-cross abaci, various multi-scalloped capitals, decorative string courses, capitals with plain and beaded cable necking, and vault responds with coursed angle shafts (figs.1-7). The foliage on the right main shaft of the south doorway relates to the abacus of the second capital in the north nave arcade in the cathedral. Furthermore, on this cathedral capital there are beaded medallions, two of which are joined by a grotesque mask and two which contain creatures as on the outer order of the south doorway at Kilpeck. More generally, the three-dimensional lozenged chevron on the Kilpeck apse ribs, while not identical to any specific form at the

Fig.9 Crossing arch at Hereford Cathedral

13

Fig.10 Capital in the eastern niche of Hereford Cathedral's south transept which is a coarser version of the human-headed corbels at Kilpeck

cathedral, belongs to the same family (figs.2 & 9).

These parallels suggest that there is a very close relationship between the architectural ornament at Kilpeck and that at the cathedral. However, it is not so straighforward for the figurative work. The human-headed corbels with moustaches growing from the sides of the nose are refined versions of the one on the left capital in the eastern niche of the cathedral south transept (figs.10, 111, 117, & 118). The striated, cap-like hair and huge bulbous eyes of the top left Kilpeck chancel arch figure are presaged by the flying angel on the capital of the east presbytery arch (figs.11 & 121). The Hereford heads lack the finesse of those at Kilpeck, but this is not surprising since the Hereford angel (fig.11), along with the other capitals of the presbytery east arch, would have been executed soon after the start of the cathedral, around 1107-15, some 20 to 30 years before the work at Kilpeck. Perhaps Hereford Cathedral provided the initial training ground for sculptors who later worked in the Herefordshire School.

One capital at Hereford Cathedral, now lost, was recorded by the Royal Commission.[11] Their illustration shows two winged quadrupeds with scaly bodies on one face and on the left creature the form of the head with gaping mouth and huge eye matches well the sculptures at Kilpeck. Specifically, the scaly bodies relate to Kilpeck corbel No.4 (fig.64), while the head with gaping mouth and huge eye relates to the same corbel and the basilisk on the left capital of the south doorway (fig.56). This capital from Hereford Cathedral topped a free-standing shaft and probably came from a sub-division of a gallery arch. It provides the most specific evidence that one of the Kilpeck sculptors, probably the Chief Master, worked at Hereford Cathedral before Kilpeck.

Fig.11 The flying angel capital from the east presbytery arch at Hereford Cathedral

It has been convincingly argued that the carved figures on the Kilpeck chancel arch are similar in design to the figure of God painted in the initial to Hosea, V in a manuscript almost certainly produced in Hereford in the second quarter of the twelfth century (*see rear cover*).[12] However, there is no way of telling whether the Hereford manuscript influenced the Kilpeck sculpture or *vice versa*.

Influence of St Peter's Gloucester

Apart from Hereford, parallels for architectural and sculptural details at Kilpeck have been found in various parts of Gloucester Cathedral, from blind arches at the east end, to features in the nave and chapter house, and fragments without exact provenance but which may come from the Romanesque cloister or west front. The continuous roll moulding of the apse windows derives from Gloucester, where it is used to articulate the exterior of each side of the upper storey of the polygonal radiating and transept chapels.[13] The 90-degree chevron on both the chancel arch and the south doorway at Kilpeck, in which there are two narrow steps, a thick roll and then a thin step, is precisely paralleled in the north nave arcade at Gloucester (figs.5 & 12). Similarly, the chevron on the north-east and south-east ribs of the apse vault at Kilpeck has a central band of continuous lozenges framed with single zigzaged angle rolls just as in the two east arches of the blind arcade reused on the south-east 'bridge' at Gloucester.[14] The form of the responds—the half pillars backing onto walls and which support ribs—of the Kilpeck apse with angle rolls to the pilaster is paralleled in the blind arcade of the Gloucester chapter house.[15] It is even possible that the juxtaposition of a barrel vault and a ribbed apsidal sanctuary reflects the scheme of the Romanesque sanctuary at Gloucester.[16]

*Fig.12 Detail of arch architectural mouldings of westernmost bay
in north nave arcade in Gloucester Cathedral*

Fig.13 Apse boss, Kilpeck

Fig.14 Voussoir Nos.13 & 14, Kilpeck

Fig.15 Head from Gloucester Cathedral now in St John's Cathedral, Newfoundland

Figurative and foliage sculpture in both places confirm the architectural links. The head at the apex of the westernmost bay of the Romanesque north nave arcade at Gloucester belongs to the same family as those on the Kilpeck south doorway and apse boss (figs. 12 & 13). For instance, the bulbous eyeballs with drilled pupils; the angular section of the pronounced eyelids; the radial delineation of the eyebrows; the small, cat-like ears; and the long snout of the Gloucester head are all found on the first head on the right of the middle order of the Kilpeck south doorway (voussoir No.14), and, minus the long snout, on voussoir No.5 (figs.12, 14 & 20). The fleshier forms of the corbel from Gloucester, preserved in the Anglican Cathedral at St Johns, Newfoundland, are allied to the masks that link the medallions of the outer order of the Kilpeck doorway (fig.15).[17] There is a fragment of a similar label stop at Gloucester which, like Kilpeck corbel No.69 (fig.106), devours a human head.[18] The two-and three-strand stems with binding ties and spiralled and lobed foliage terminations on the central capital of the westernmost north nave aisle respond at Gloucester are allied to the panels behind the dragons' heads at the south-east, south-west and north-west angles of the Kilpeck nave.[19]

St Peter's, Gloucester, was commenced in 1089 and was dedicated in 1100. The huge columnar piers of the nave show distinct marks of fire damage and this is presumably associated with the fire of 1122.[20] Whether the nave was completed or was still under construction at this date is debatable. However, it may be significant that foliated capitals are only introduced towards the completion of the building of the west end of the north nave aisle, just as the figurated capitals at nearby Tewkesbury Abbey are first used towards the west end of the north nave triforium.[21] Tewkesbury was commenced about 1087; the monks moved into the church in 1102, and there was a dedication in 1123.[22] The parallel chronology of Tewkesbury and Gloucester, along with the architectural similarities between the two buildings, may suggest that the introduction of more richly decorated capitals in a part of the nave with no obvious liturgical significance came at the same time in both buildings. There are no constructional dates for the chapter house or Romanesque cloister at Gloucester, but it is likely that they were being built at the same time as the nave, although work on the richly decorated cloister could have continued into the 1130s. The documented gift of Kilpeck to Gloucester in 1134 suggests that work on Kilpeck took place after that at Gloucester.

It could therefore be inferred that Gloucester-trained craftsmen were employed in the design and execution of Kilpeck, especially as there are other links between churches associated with Gloucester Abbey and Kilpeck.

A small fragment of a figurated capital at Tewkesbury Abbey is carved with a human head in profile, broken off just below the eye with striated ribbons of hair,[23] like a more detailed version of St Peter on the Kilpeck chancel arch (fig.119). In front of his head there is what appears to be his arm which is covered with ringed cloth as on the knights of the Kilpeck south doorway (fig.36). Is he in a jockey-like pose on a horse? The figures are set beneath an arch with a cable moulding in the soffit as on the string course beneath the west

Fig.106 (left) Corbel no.69 at Kilpeck compared with Fig.16 (above) a capital in the north nave triforium at Tewkesbury Abbey

17

window at Kilpeck (fig.55). Connections are also evident between the Tewkesbury north nave triforium capitals and Kilpeck. In particular, in the capital of the eastern arch of the second bay from the west, the south-west angle cat's head devours a human head in the manner of Kilpeck corbel No.69 (figs.106 & 16). On the eastern

Fig.17 Capital in north nave triforium of Tewkesbury Abbey

capital of the western bay of the north nave triforium at Tewkesbury the man wears flared, ribbed, three-quarter-length trousers like the knights on Kilpeck corbels No.7 and No.10 (figs.17 & 66). In view of the close architectural connections between Tewkesbury and Gloucester, it is reasonable to assume that the same sculptors would have worked in both places. How one wishes that more of the Tewkesbury cloister sculpture had been preserved.

Just to the east of Hereford, Dormington Church belonged to St Peter's, Gloucester. The knocker on the south door of Dormington's church (fig.18), has long been associated with the sculpture of the Herefordshire School (Beckwith 1956) and in particular may be compared with Kilpeck corbel No.69 (figs.106, & 18) and also with the Gloucester label stop. Both the knocker and the Gloucester Candlestick (now in the Victoria and Albert Museum) were probably made at Gloucester Abbey.[24] The candlestick, which was commissioned by Abbot Peter of Gloucester (1107-1113), has been cited as an example of the type of metalwork to which the Kilpeck sculptors may have turned for inspiration.[25] Certainly, on the candlestick there are both beaded and striated stems to the foliage, as at Kilpeck, and some of the human and grotesque heads bear a certain family resemblance to Kilpeck. However, the parallels are not sufficiently

Fig.18 Doorknocker at Dormington Church

18

close to suggest that the Herefordshire sculptors made direct reference to the candlestick. Be that as it may, Lawrence Stone's observation that the prominent ankle bones of the Kilpeck chancel arch figures may well reproduce in stone the original nails that attached a bronze figure to the background of a shrine, reredos or altar frontal,[26] strongly suggests that the art of the metalworker was a formative influence on the Kilpeck sculpture.

The formal connections between Kilpeck and Gloucester are at once promising and frustrating. On the one hand, parallels between the grotesque heads suggest that master craftsmen might have worked in both places. On the other hand, to establish such a fundamental link on the basis of just two heads at Gloucester is asking a lot. It is at a moment like this that one wonders what the west front and cloister of Romanesque Gloucester looked like.

Works in Gloucestershire related to St Peter's and Kilpeck

Land at Forthampton was given to Tewkesbury Abbey in 1107 and construction of St Mary's Church appears to have begun about this time.[27] Apart from the

The mask at the apex of the south doorway at Forthampton, Gloucestershire, (Fig.19 above left) is positioned in the same way as the head at the apex on the westernmost Romanesque north nave arcade arch at Gloucester (fig.12) and is stylistically related both to it and to some of the Kilpeck south doorway voussoirs (Fig.20 and Fig.21 above right)

connections with the apex mask (see figs.19-21 previous page) it is also significant that on the Forthampton arch there are dragon's head label stops, as well as beaded medallions like those at Hereford, Llandaff and Sarum Cathedrals.[28]

An apex mask, which is very close to the masks linking the medallions on the right of the outer order of Kilpeck's south doorway, also appears reset on the west wall of the chancel above the chancel arch at Upleadon in Gloucestershire (figs.33 & 22).

Here the connection with Gloucester Abbey is confirmed through the inclusion of truncated cones in the hollow roll beneath the head, exactly as in the cathedral's north nave arcade arch.

On the former south doorway of the chapel of St Mary Magdalen, Wootton, the tympanum is plain, but is framed with roll mouldings as at Kilpeck.[29] The top of the left

Fig.22 Label mask reset above the chancel arch at Upleadon, Gloucestershire

capital of the Wootton doorway is adorned with stylized flowers, an unusual feature but one paralleled on two of the north nave aisle responds at Gloucester Cathedral.[30] The beaded and two-strand stems, binding ties and asymmetrical trilobe leaves on the Wootton left capital are similar to the foliage on the Kilpeck tympanum (fig.5).[31]

Several aspects of the sculpture at St John's, Elkstone belong to the same family as Gloucester and Kilpeck. The south doorway has an apex mask and, on the inner order, two masks—the second and fifth from the right—which are close to the voussoirs (Nos.4 and 9) on the middle order of Kilpeck south doorway (fig.5).[32] The boss of the Elkstone chancel rib vault has four grotesque masks in the manner of the Kilpeck apse vault (figs.13 & 23), while the label of the chancel arch is carved with balls—as on the central capital of respond 7 of the north nave aisle at Gloucester Cathedral—and is terminated on dragon's head stops. The connections between Elkstone and Kilpeck are probably not direct and instead reflect a common heritage, possibly the lost cloister or west front of St Peter's, Gloucester?

The Dymock and Herefordshire Schools
The importance of the Dymock School for the carvings at Kilpeck was established by Zarnecki.[33] Some unusual technical details serve to emphasise this

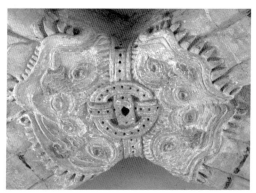

Fig.23 Sanctuary vault boss at Elkstone Church, Gloucestershire

link. The lower half of the Kilpeck tympanum is carved from the same stone as the lintel and the latter extends laterally below the roll mouldings that frame the tympanum (fig.5). The roll mouldings are carved on regular wedge-shaped voussoirs. A similar arrangement occurs in the south doorway at Pauntley, Gloucestershire, where the lowest sections of the rolls surrounding the tympanum are cut from the same stone as the tympanum itself (figs.5 & 24). The decoration of the lintel is also carved on the same stone and is confined to the section beneath the tympanum, while the areas below the roll mouldings are left plain as at Kilpeck. The upper section of the tympanum at Pauntley is also carved from two pieces of stone as at Kilpeck.

Details of the chancel arch at Pauntley also relate to Kilpeck. The chip-carved, saltire crosses on the inner order of the Pauntley arch are like those on the capitals of the Kilpeck south doorway (fig.5), while the raised semi-circles on the capitals at Pauntley also appear on the Kilpeck chancel arch. The heads on the capitals of the outer order of the Pauntley arch are not directly paralleled at Kilpeck. However, their wide-eyed stare and clearly defined facial features compare favourably with those on many of the Kilpeck corbels, while the two-strand stems below and to the sides of the heads are reminiscent of the nest of the phoenix on Kilpeck's south doorway (fig.60).

Fig.24 South Doorway to Pauntley Church, Gloucestershire

The heads of the window in the south wall and the west window in the north wall of the nave at Kilpeck are cut from single stones and incised with imitation voussoirs in the manner of the blocked doorway to the former stair in the axial tower at Dymock.[34] Certain stones of the pilaster buttresses at Kilpeck continue into the rubble masonry of the wall as at Dymock.[35] This

Fig.25 The South Doorway at Kilpeck

Fig.26 (Top left) North doorway of All Saints Church at Laughton-en-le-Morthen, Yorkshire

Fig.27 (Top right) North doorway of St Patrick's Chapel, Heysham, Lancashire

Fig.28 North doorway of All Saints, Somerford Keynes, Gloucestershire

technique is generally associated with pre-Conquest churches and as such serves to introduce other elements at Kilpeck which reflect an Anglo-Saxon tradition.[36]

The points of similarity between Kilpeck and the Dymock school are predominantly ones of masonry technique and geometric ornament. With the possible exception of the masks on the capitals of the Pauntley chancel arch, there is nothing to suggest that any of the master sculptors worked in the churches of the Dymock School.

Kilpeck and links with Anglo-Saxon and Celtic Traditions

On the Kilpeck south doorway, the disjunction between the imposts of the inner order and the abaci of the capitals which carry both the second and third orders is alien to a logically ordered Norman approach but is akin to the Anglo-Saxon north nave doorway at Laughton-en-le-Morthen, Yorkshire (figs.25 & 26). The thin roll mouldings that surround the tympanum at Kilpeck recall pre-Conquest works like the west doorway of All Saints, Earls Barton in Northamptonshire;

the north doorway of St Patrick's Chapel at Heysham, Lancashire; and the north doorway of All Saints, Somerford Keynes, Gloucestershire (figs.5, 27 & 28). At Somerford Keynes the mouldings have a rope ornament unlike the plain rolls at Kilpeck, but just like Kilpeck the Somerford Keynes doorway has a plain area above the moulded imposts before the start of the arch mouldings.

The carved, monolithic jambs of the Kilpeck south doorway are unusual in a Romanesque building and may reflect the pre-Conquest tradition of carved crosses notably in Wales, as in the Llandough, Glamorganshire, pillar (fig.29).[37] Alternatively, the style could be an adaptation of a tradition in wooden sculpture as represented in the door jambs of Norwegian stave churches.[38] Given the formal relationship between the dragons' heads that project from the west wall at Kilpeck (fig.7), with both the heads on the Anglo-Saxon west tower at Deerhurst, and with the heads on the gable ends of stave churches, one may ask to what extent the Kilpeck decoration might have reflected that of wooden Anglo-Saxon churches? Unfortunately, with the loss of all the English wooden churches, this theory cannot be tested. Nevertheless, one circumstantial clue can be found to support it. The copper alloy Pershore censer-cover[39] is capped with a 'Rhenish-Helm' spire, reminiscent of the west tower of Sompting, Sussex, with 'wooden' shingles and beasts' heads projecting from the gable ends.[40] While the Sompting spire may not be Anglo-Saxon in date it most likely represents a pre-Conquest tradition. The fusion of wooden and stone architectural elements in the Pershore censer cover highlights the importance of inter-media relationships in medieval art, which must be borne in mind when considering the sources for the motifs on the Kilpeck south doorway.

Fig.29 Llandough Pillar, Glamorgan

As an example, the dragon's head with interlaced body at the right springer of the inner order of the doorway closely resembles patterns on small metal objects which belong to the so-called Salin Style II.[41] The beaded interlaced body of the animal on the left capital finds a counterpart in the seventh- or eighth-century Hunterstone brooch.[42] The form of the fifth beakhead from the left resembles the head of a bronze 'spur' with its emerging conical pointed rod in the Ashmolean Museum, Oxford.[43] On corbel No.10 on the nave south wall the arms of the two men facing each other are interlaced in the manner of early medieval animal ornament of the type well-known with the Sutton Hoo Great Gold Buckle and Purse Lid.[44]

Whether such parallels demonstrate that the Kilpeck sculptors derived motifs directly from pre-Conquest metalwork is difficult to establish. Given the similarity between the Kilpeck and Deerhurst dragon's head stops (figs.30 & 31) and the head terminals on the Runic-inscribed mount from the River

Thames,[45] the possibility that motifs were already integrated into monumental carving before the Conquest must remain open.

Numerous pre-Conquest sources may be cited for the ribbed draperies of the Kilpeck knights as on the Aghadoe crozier preserved in Stockholm National Museum.[46] Ultimately the motif may derive from a Celtic tradition as represented by such works as the late second/early first-century B.C. Gundestrup Caldron, on which the figure in question is further allied to Kilpeck in the form of the egg-shaped head, the bulbous eyes and neatly combed, cap-like hair.[47] Ribbed draperies may also reflect regional Roman sculpture.

Connections between Kilpeck and Romano-British Sculpture

The votive tablet to Romulus in the form of Mars, preserved in the Gloucester City Museum, has ribbed draperies like the Kilpeck south doorway knights (fig.25).

A head from the Bon Marché site in Gloucester, which is now preserved in the Gloucester City Museum, has been dated to both the mid-first century A.D. and the twelfth century. The ultimate

Fig.30 (above) Dragon's head stop on the south doorway at Kilpeck
Fig.31 (lower) Label stop on interior of west nave doorway at Deerhurst, Gloucestershire

Celtic ancestry of features like the narrow, tapering face and the huge, projecting eyeballs is without dispute. However, the hair style has been seen as both an imitation of Julio-Claudian portraits,[48] and compared with sculpture characteristic of the Herefordshire School.[49] Bulbous eyes and glum expressions are indeed common to the Bon Marché and Kilpeck chancel arch heads, but in the latter the modelling is more plastic, especially for the cheekbones (figs.119-122). This is not to deny the connection between the Bon Marché head and the Herefordshire School, for a thinner, tapering, less-modelled face is found on the knights of the Kilpeck south doorway (fig.36) and on corbel No.77 (fig.110) on the nave west wall at Kilpeck. Whether the Bon Marché head dates from the first or the twelfth century is difficult to decide; that it has been dated to both periods and allied in particular with the Herefordshire School serves to emphasise the potential of regional Roman sculpture as one of the sources for the Romanesque sculptors of Kilpeck and the Herefordshire School.

Santiago de Compostella and/or Ferrara

The superposed figures on the shafts of the chancel arch at Kilpeck are unusual but find general comparison in the marble shafts of the Puerta de las Platerias, the south transept doorway, of the great pilgrimage church at Santiago de Compostella.[50] The placement of the Kilpeck chancel arch figures has also been compared with the west portal of Ferrara Cathedral.[51] The Ferrara figures are cut from the square jambs of the portal rather than the shafts as at Kilpeck. However, it may be significant that, as on the Kilpeck south doorway, there is a similar disjunction between the capitals that support the lintel and those of the other orders of the Ferrara portal. Furthermore, is it more than coincidence that the then unusual theme of St George killing the dragon is used on the tympanum at Ferrara and also in the Herefordshire School at Brinsop and Ruardean?

It is documented that Oliver de Merlimond, the patron of Shobdon Church, went on a pilgrimage to Santiago de Compostella, and it can be deduced that he returned through western France. This is normally taken to account for the connection between Kilpeck, western France and Santiago de Compostella. It is most likely that Oliver's pilgrimage was undertaken between 1125 and 1130,[52] but the event is not precisely dated and may not have happened until work at Kilpeck was already underway or even finished. The possibility therefore remains that Hugh of Kilpeck, or one of his relations or associates, was responsible for the connection between Kilpeck, western France and Santiago de Compostella. Moreover, if the link with Ferrara is valid then pilgrimage to Rome, which would have involved travel along the Via Emilia, would have also allowed discussion of church sculpture with fellow travellers and even the

Western France

The figurated medallions of Kilpeck's south doorway may be compared with the west window of Notre-Dame-la-Grande, Poitiers (*figs.5 & 35 (middle right)*). Similarly, voussoirs No.2 and No.12 of the middle order of the Kilpeck south doorway, with dragons turning to bite their own tails, are allied to the outer order of the west doorway of this Poitiers church (*figs.32, 33 (top left and top right) & 34 (middle right)*). The superposed figures on the main left shaft of the south doorway at Kilpeck, a very unusual motif, are paralleled on the west portal at Maillezais, Vendée (*figs.36 (lower left) & 37 (lower right)*). There are also similarities in subject matter between the Kilpeck corbels and those in western France at Matha-Marestay.

production of quick sketches. Once again, dating is not a straightforward matter. The Ferrara portal was probably completed by 1135, when the bishop moved into the newly consecrated cathedral.[53] Therefore, for the link between Kilpeck and Ferrara to be substantiated, it would have to be argued that the Ferrara portal was sufficiently advanced by the early 1130s to have inspired a visitor from Herefordshire.

The connections with Reading Abbey

Reading Abbey, which was founded by King Henry I in 1121, has been seen as an important source for Kilpeck and the Herefordshire School.[54] Indeed, it has even been seen as the primary inspiration for the motifs of the school,[55] though few would support such a radical view.[56]

However, there are undeniable similarities between Kilpeck and Reading. The beakhead on voussoir No.10 of the second order of the Kilpeck south doorway is closely paralleled at Reading Abbey.[57] The inhabited, beaded medallions on the outer order of the south doorway at Kilpeck recall those on a fragmentary shaft from Reading.[58] A capital from Reading with two winged, seated, haloed figures also recalls Kilpeck. Specifically, the heads with cap-like hair and huge bulbous eyes are like the Kilpeck chancel arch figures, while the ribbed draperies relate to the knights on the south doorway. Even closer to the Kilpeck chancel arch figures are two heads on the south capital of the western crossing arch of St Mary's, Cholsey, Berkshire, a church that belonged to Reading Abbey (fig.38). Also at Cholsey is a loose capital decorated with both beaded and incised stems as on the Kilpeck tympanum (figs.5 & 39).

The eastern arch of the north nave arcade of St Mary's, English Bicknor, Gloucestershire, is carved with beakheads which have been related to Kilpeck.[59]

Fig.38 (left) Crossing arch capital and Fig.39 (above) Loose capital, both at Cholsey Church, Berkshire

The connection between English Bicknor, Reading Abbey and Kilpeck is supported by comparing Kilpeck corbel No.30 (fig.87 above left) with the third beakhead from the left on the English Bicknor arch (Fig.40 above right). However, the English Bicknor heads lack the quality of Kilpeck

The manor of English Bicknor was granted to Miles of Gloucester by Henry I, probably in 1131.[60] This grant and Miles' close association with the king may explain the relationship between the beakheads of English Bicknor and Reading Abbey, though the link with Kilpeck, if any, is difficult to determine. The juxta-position of the heads to the roll and hollow moulding and the chevron ornament are identical in both places and suggests some sort of connection.

Understanding these parallels is not straightforward. For example, beaded roundels were also used as part of the decorative repertoire at Reading.[61] This motif had already appeared at Hereford Cathedral and Forthampton before Reading was commenced. It was also used on the eastern arch and the south window of the presbytery at Llandaff Cathedral sometime after 1120 (fig.41). Architectural features like cylindrical piers with single shafts attached towards the aisle in the presbytery of Reading Abbey come from a West Country Romanesque style at Evesham Abbey, while the elongated crossing piers at Reading are ubiquitous in the major Romanesque churches of the west country school as at Gloucester and Tewkesbury.[62] Thus, there is influence from the west country school on Reading Abbey as well as the other way round. Be that as it may, whatever precise connections there may be between sculptural motifs of Reading Abbey and Kilpeck, there can be no doubt that the unprecedented wealth of sculpture at Reading provided inspiration for the richness of Kilpeck.

Fig.41 South window of the presbytery at Llandaff Cathedral

Hugh of Kilpeck clearly wished to emulate the most prestigious works of his time and to be seen as a man of regal taste through the enrichment of his church at Kilpeck.

Links with Old Sarum Cathedral

It has also been suggested that certain motifs found at Kilpeck reflect the decoration of Old Sarum Cathedral under the patronage of Bishop Roger (1103-1139).[63] Indeed, there are many similarities between the Kilpeck and Sarum sculpture. The rosette on Kilpeck corbel No.22 (fig.75) also appears in a roundel from Sarum reused in the east wall of Salisbury Cathedral Close (fig.42).[64] Both may reflect a common origin in western France (fig.76),but the connection between Kilpeck and Sarum seems to be confirmed by the stunning similarity of Kilpeck corbel No.38 to the head on a corbel from Sarum Cathedral preserved in the Salisbury and South Wiltshire Museum (figs.67 and 43).[65] Both heads compare favourably to a loose corbel of a mouth puller in the Victoria and Albert Museum[66] which Paul

Fig.42 Roundel from Sarum Cathedral

Williamson[67] has compared with both Kilpeck and Sarum. A corbel carved with a crouching figure blowing a horn from Sarum Cathedral, now in the Salisbury and South Wiltshire Museum, is also closely allied to Kilpeck (fig.44). In particular, the shape of the head of the horn blower relates to the female exhibitionist and the dancers corbels at Kilpeck (Nos.28 & 45, figs.78 & 92), while the treatment of the eyes of the Kilpeck female exhibitionist is a simplified version of this Sarum corbel.

The Sarum sculpture is not precisely dated. Whilst King tells us

The marked similarity between corbel No.38 at Kilpeck (Fig.86 (left))
and a head on a corbel from Sarum Cathedral (Fig.43 (right))

that 'much of the new east end [of Sarum Cathedral] was already complete by 1125',[68] and cites William of Malmesbury's comment that 'documents testify [it] was begun during the first quarter of the twelfth century',[69] the work was still incomplete at the time of Bishop Roger's death in 1139.[70]

Further comparisons between Sarum, Kilpeck and works in Gloucestershire attest to the complexity in deciphering the progression of styles. A grotesque mask possibly from the lower section of a round window at Sarum, also in the Salisbury and South Wiltshire Museum (fig.46),[71] is allied to several heads on the middle order of the Kilpeck south doorway with their almond-shaped eyes with small drilled pupils, and finely scored eyebrows (figs.14, 20 & 46). At the same time this Sarum head

Fig.44 A corbel from Sarum Cathedral related to corbels at Kilpeck

31

Fig.45 (left) A label mask from Sarum preserved in the Salisbury and South Wiltshire Museum relates closely to the apse vault boss at Kilpeck (fig.13 (right))

and the label mask belong to the same family as the label masks at Gloucester Cathedral, Forthampton and Upleadon (figs.12, 19, 45 & 46). This raises the possibility that the motifs disseminated from Gloucester.

Whatever final judgment is reached on the movement of sculptors between Sarum, Gloucester, Kilpeck and related works, it is important to remember that, like the work for the king at Reading Abbey, the decoration of Bishop Roger's Sarum Cathedral set a new standard for richly decorated churches. As such it was an appropriate model for an ambitious patron like Hugh of Kilpeck.

Fig.46 Voussoir from Sarum Cathedral

CHAPTER 3

The Sculptors

Whilst a fair amount is known about the patrons, their taste and their intellectual background, it is less easy to discover information about the sculptors.

The training of a mason or sculptor involved apprenticeship in a mason's yard. Documentary sources indicate that masons were associated with major ecclesiastical establishments. Blithere, the master mason of Abbot Scotland's church of St Augustine at Canterbury, is described in 1091 as 'the very distinguished master of the beautiful church.'[1] Harvey suggests that Blithere is to be identified with the Blittaere or Blize who, according to Domesday (3.10), held Seasalter, Kent, of the monks of Christ Church, Canterbury. Robert the Mason (fl. *c*.1077-1119) at St Albans is described as excelling all masons at his time.[2] He was given a house in St Albans and lands for his good service to the abbey, probably as master mason of the Romanesque abbey church. According to Hampshire Domesday (3.1), Hugh the Mason held land for two ploughs which had belonged to one Giraud in Chilcomb near Winchester, a manor in the hands of Walkelin, Bishop of Winchester (1070-98). Harvey equates Hugh with the master mason of the Romanesque fabric of Winchester Cathedral.[3] Herefordshire Domesday records (2.27) that an anonymous mason (*caementarius*) was rewarded by Robert of Lorraine, Bishop of Hereford (1079-95), with a hide and half a virgate at Eastnor. Perhaps he was the master mason of Bishop Robert's chapel at Hereford, for this holding compares favourably with the two priests at Fownhope who held half a hide of land.[4] These rewards establish a respected status in society. Further, the reward of the master mason with gifts from the church suggests a permanence in the relationship, given the large size of the project and the prolonged building activity, including control over a large workforce.

The qualitative differences between the Herefordshire School sculptures, so obvious in the corbels at Kilpeck, would have been similarly reflected in the remuneration and status of the sculptors.

Professor Zarnecki[5] has suggested that there were two major personalities amongst the sculptors, the Chief Master, whose bold style is represented by the figures on the chancel arch at Kilpeck, and the Aston Master, who was given his name from his early work on the sculpture at St Giles at Aston and whose more restrained hand is detected in the medallions on the outer order of the south doorway at Kilpeck.[6] Zarnecki also suggested that the Chief Master and Aston Master worked together at Shobdon Church before moving to Kilpeck. To trace the hand of the Chief Master and the Aston Master through several buildings and to find a sculptor at work at Monmouth Castle chapel suggests the sculptors worked in a professional long-term capacity.

Was there a division of roles between sculptor and mason in the workshop? There can be little doubt that the top men, the Chief Master and the Aston Master, were involved solely with the sculptural decoration. In the case of the Aston Master, this is suggested by comparison of Aston and Rock, two churches where his hand is detected, but where there are totally different building techniques. Aston is built of rubble with cut-stone, non-projecting quoins and no buttresses, whilst Rock is built of ashlar and with pilaster buttresses. Similarly for the Chief Master; at Kilpeck roughly squared stones are used for the apse but rubble for the chancel and nave except for the windows and buttresses, while at Leominster fine ashlar construction is used throughout the priory church. Differentiation of tasks is also suggested by comparison of Kilpeck with the churches at Moccas and Peterchurch. All three churches were probably the work of the same masons but the plainness of Moccas and Peterchurch contrasts with the exuberance of Kilpeck. The inescapable conclusion is that major sculptors were specialists and that there was a differentiation between master sculptor and master mason/architect, exactly as recorded on an inscription on the Romanesque church at Chadenac, Charente-Maritime.[7] This inscription reads (in translation): 'Here lies William the Poitevin clerk of William / The architect, but not the sculptor.'

What tools were used? Writing in the late twelfth century, the chronicler monk, Gervase of Canterbury, contrasts the Romanesque capitals in the cathedral, which were carved with an axe, with the rich acanthus capitals of the early Gothic eastern arm (1175-84), which were executed with a chisel.[8] Clearly this cannot be taken to mean that all Romanesque sculpture was axe-carved, for the detailing of Kilpeck south doorway, for example, makes it clear that the chisel and drill must have been employed in the work.

Was the sculpture carved in the workshop and then set into position, or was it carved *in situ*, in other words after the stones had been placed in position. Medieval illustrations of sculptors at work show them carving the stone on the bench in the workshop. The degree to which carving was executed *in situ* has been, and doubtless will continue to be, a matter of debate, as with the celebrated case of the doorways of the Lady Chapel at Glastonbury Abbey.[9] At the very least some finishing would have been done *in situ*, as with the Kilpeck and Aston tympana with their odd-shaped stones. At Lincoln, the frieze on the cathedral's west front may well be contemporary with the facade it occupies (1072/5-92) and yet the sculpture on it is difficult to explain stylistically before the 1140s; carving *in situ* seems to be a plausible solution to the dilemma.

Where were the Herefordshire sculptors trained? It is here that the losses amongst the twelfth-century great churches of Herefordshire and Gloucestershire make things very difficult. At Leominster Priory there is the matter of the cloister, long cited as the possible lost intermediary between the sculpture of the mother house at Reading and the Herefordshire School.[10] St Guthlac's Priory at Hereford was a daughter house of St Peter's, Gloucester, and was richly endowed by the Lacy family but nothing remains of it. Kilpeck, Dormington and Castle Frome were also given to St Peter's, Gloucester. This association would suggest that, notably, the Kilpeck sculptures would owe much to Gloucester. But the loss of the Romanesque cloister and the west front of St Peter's, the total loss of Winchcombe Abbey, and the survival of just a few mangled fragments from the cloister at Tewkesbury Abbey, make it difficult to assess whether this is the case. However, tracing the styles and work suggests that the Chief Master received his early training in the workshop at Hereford Cathedral. He almost certainly worked at Tewkesbury Abbey, possibly at St Peter's Gloucester, and even at Old Sarum Cathedral. For the Aston Master involvement at Hereford Cathedral seems to be certain.

The Bromyard or Dymock School was important for supplying the training for the masons and the carvers of ornament but, with the possible exception of the chancel arch capitals at Pauntley, there is nothing to indicate that either the Chief Master or the Aston Master worked in the churches of the Dymock School.

The Dormington door knocker, the Deposition ivory (fig.241) and Hereford Cathedral MS. P.4.iii suggest connections between the Herefordshire School, especially the Chief Master, and centres of sumptuous art production at Gloucester and Hereford. Metalworking details, as suggested by parallels between the Dormington door knocker and the Kilpeck corbels, along with Stone's observation that the oversize ankle bones of the Kilpeck chancel arch figures may derive from the nails used to attach metal figures to wooden panels, indicate some of the sculptors had been metalworkers.[11] The figures on St Manchan's Shrine, Boher (Co. Offaly),[12] relate to the chancel arch figures at Kilpeck and, along with the other parallels, suggest that the Chief Master may have practised as a metalworker, like Master Hugo of Bury St Edmunds. Master Hugo, best known for his 'incomparably painted' Bury Bible,[13] cast a bell and made the bronze doors of the abbey in the time of Abbot Anselm (1121-48), and carved a cross in the choir with figures of St John and the Virgin (1148-56). 'As in other works he surpassed everyone else, so in making these gates he surpassed himself.'[14]

CHAPTER 4

Kilpeck

The village of Kilpeck lies eight miles south-west of Hereford just to the south of the A465. Its parish church of St Mary and St David has been described as 'one of the most perfect Norman village churches in England' (fig.47),[1] whilst it also lies towards one end of a deserted medieval village site. It is a classic example of a Romanesque three-cell plan with a stilted apsidal sanctuary, square chancel, and rectangular nave. This twelfth-century fabric has undergone only minor changes; the priest's door in the south wall of the chancel is Gothic, and there are single Gothic windows in the north and south walls of the chancel and in the eastern bay of the north nave wall. The belfry belongs to Cottingham's restoration but it is archaeologically so accurate a creation as to convince most viewers that it is a twelfth-century original. The church is exceptional for the sculpture lavished on the south doorway, the chancel arch, and the west window. In addition, there are dragons' heads projecting from the west wall and the south-east angle of the nave, a carved corbels round the entire church, and masks on the boss of the apse vault.

The church lies just to the east of the castle, of which the motte and a fragment of the keep survive. We have indeed 'one of the classic examples of a planned medieval settlement laid out next to a Norman castle.'[2] The close juxtaposition of church and castle conforms to a standard Norman practice. It is witnessed on the largest scale with the cathedral and castle, as at Durham, Lincoln or Norwich.[3] Castle and monastic church are often paired as at Castle Acre, Norfolk; Chepstow and Usk Monmouthshire; or castle and a small collegiate or parish church as at Bramber, Sussex, and Castle Rising, Norfolk. In each case they stood as powerful symbols of Norman control over both the secular and religious life of the community.

Fig.47 Church of St Mary and St David, Kilpeck

Kilpeck Priory (the church being an endowment of the priory) was given by Hugh, lord of Kilpeck Castle and son of William fitz Norman, to St Peter's Abbey (now cathedral), Gloucester, in 1134.[4] There is good reason to believe that the church was completed by that date, for the disruption in the region caused by the Welsh rebellion and civil war following the death of King Henry I in 1135 was hardly conducive to the commencement of a new church.[5]

Description

The church is built of Old Red Sandstone and is divided into three separate spaces (fig.47). At the east end there is the stilted, semi-circular apse which is built of roughly squared stones (fig.48). There is a string course below the apse windows at sill level which is not continued in the chancel and nave. In contrast to the otherwise rough masonry, ashlar (neatly finished, squared stonework) is used for the pilaster buttresses and the round-headed windows. The construction of the buttresses is unusual in that certain stones extend from the buttress into the face of the wall. The windows have arched heads formed from single stones and have continuous roll mouldings.

The chancel is built of rubble masonry rather than the small, squared stones used for the apse, although the ashlar pilaster buttresses at the eastern angles and in the middle of the north and south walls take on the same form as in the

38

Fig.48 The apse at Kilpeck Church

apse. The cornice is ornamented with a roll moulding topped with a row of beads on the flat face.

The importance of the apse is established with both the internal and external arrangement. The use of a vault in the apse of an otherwise wood-roofed church goes back to the Early Christian basilica where it took the form of a semi-dome above the high altar to represent the dome of heaven. This iconography is upheld and elaborated at Kilpeck with the inclusion of ribs in the vault, for they are ultimately related to those in the *baldacchino* over the shrine of St Peter in the Constantinian church of Old St Peter's, Rome.[6] The rib was introduced into English architecture after the Conquest. At Durham Cathedral (1093) it was used throughout the church thereby creating a monumental shrine for their most famous relic, the body of St Cuthbert.[7] Relevant to Kilpeck, is the selective use of the rib within the sanctuary, as in the apsidal chapel of the south transept at Tewkesbury Abbey (after 1087), in the apses of the transept crypts and south transept chapel at Christchurch (Twyneham) Priory (*c*.1090), formerly in the main apse and forebay at Peterborough Cathedral (formerly abbey) (1117/18), and in the eastern bay of the chancel at Ewenny Priory, Glamorganshire (1116-26).[8] In each of these cases the rib was used to signify the altar space. At Kilpeck this is enhanced by rich chevron

Fig.49 The interior of Peterchurch Church

ornament on the ribs and in the window heads, the latter standing in sharp contrast to the plain windows in the nave. On the exterior there are continuous roll mouldings to the windows and there is a string course beneath the window sills, both of which are absent in the chancel and nave. The hierarchical difference even extends to the basic building material—roughly squared, small stones for the apse as opposed to rubble for the chancel and nave .

Given this emphasis on the apse, it may seem surprising that the arch leading into it is undecorated while the arch from the nave to the chancel is so richly embellished. However, this hierarchical division is entirely purposeful—the chancel arch distinguishes the clergy area of the apse and chancel from the lay area of the nave. Its decoration indicates entry into the holier part of the building. A similar, albeit less elaborate, division occurs at Peterchurch, (fig.49).

Comparison and contrast between Kilpeck and the two other Romanesque apsidal churches in Herefordshire, at Moccas and Peterchurch, is especially

instructive. Moccas is closest in plan to Kilpeck, having three cells (figs.47 & 50), while at Peterchurch (figs.49 & 51) there is an additional cell between the chancel and nave which, as at Dymock, Gloucestershire, originally carried a tower. All three churches have stilted apses with string courses beneath the window sills. Peterchurch's apse, like Kilpeck, has pilaster buttresses and ashlar-framed windows with heads cut from single stones. Certain details support the close relationships between these three churches. For example, the chancel arch at Moccas (fig.52) has lozenge chevron like the apse ribs at Kilpeck. The chip-carved, saltire crosses of the abaci of the Kilpeck south doorway (fig.57) are also used on the Moccas chancel arch and at Peterchurch

Fig.50 (top) The three cell church at Moccas, whilst Fig.51 (lower) shows the four cell church at Peterchurch

on the tower and apse arches (fig.49). Such similarities suggest that all three churches are by the same workshop. Yet Moccas and Peterchurch do not have vaulted apses, and, with the exception of the tympana of the north and south doorways at Moccas,[9] both churches are infinitely plainer than Kilpeck. These differences cannot be attributed to differences in date; it is likely that all three churches were executed about the same time. The elaborate programme at Kilpeck would have been very expensive and therefore must represent the wishes of the patron, Hugh of Kilpeck.

Other comparisons indicate that Hugh was a patron of high standing. Similar rib-vaulted apses in three-cell Romanesque churches only occur elsewhere in England at Steetley Chapel, Derbyshire, and Birkin, Yorkshire. Like Kilpeck they both have lavish doorways. The apse of Bamburgh

Fig.52 The chancel arch at Moccas

Castle chapel, Northumberland, was also probably rib-vaulted. In Scotland there are rib-vaulted apses at Leuchars, Fife; Dalmeny and Tyningham, Lothian. The ruined hospital chapel of St James at Dunwich, Suffolk, the churches at Checkendon, Padworth and Swyncombe, Oxfordshire; Copford, Essex; Old Bewick, Northumberland; Fritton, Suffolk; and the lower chapel of Colchester Castle are all examples of vaulted apses, albeit without ribs. Of these, Copford was a chapel of the Bishop of London.[10] Colchester Castle, the largest Norman castle in England, was commenced by William I, whilst Old Bewick belonged to Tynemouth Priory, a wealthy daughter house of St Albans Abbey. Dalmeny was probably built by the wealthy Earl Gospatrick, lord of Dalmeny (d.1138), while Leuchars and Tyningham were owned by St Andrews Cathedral-Priory. These comparisons place Hugh of Kilpeck in a very select, upper echelon of patrons.

This is supported by excavation evidence from 1988/9. 'The presence of almost 200 fragments of a tile from a high-status roof of probable 12th-century date constructed of *tegulae* and *imbrices* is of great interest, especially as such a roof construction has not been recorded before in the western part of the country. It is most likely that these tiles were those used on Kilpeck Church when it was first built.'[11]

The nave, like the chancel, is rubble-built. The north wall is divided into three bays by pilaster buttresses, while on the south wall the position of the doorway occupies the place of one buttress (fig.47). At the north-east angle of the nave there is an enigmatic sloping buttress with large vertical stones and short horizontal stones, the so-called long-and-short work usually associated with the Anglo-Saxon period (fig.53). Strangely, at the top of the wall there appear to be the remains of the top of a regular twelfth-century pilaster buttress.[12] The long-and-short work is not recorded in Lewis' detailed publication of the church in 1842, his illustration and plan both showing a twelfth-century pilaster in this position.[13] It is most likely, there-fore, that the present appearance of the north-east angle of the nave is the product of restoration post Lewis but prob-ably nineteenth century. The pilaster buttresses at the other corners of the nave have panels decorated with stylized foliage at the top and projecting dragons' heads with long tongues curled in their mouths (fig.7). On the west wall next to the south dragon's head, there is also a panel carved with a relief of a dog(?) with a trefoil end to its tail (fig.54). There is another dragon's head above the pilaster buttress in the middle of the west wall. The heads of these dragons diminish in size from south to north.

Original Romanesque windows are in the first (east) bay of the nave on the south side, in the second bay on the north, and in the centre of the west front. The side windows are unmoulded, unlike the apse windows, but like the latter their arched heads are formed from single stones and in addition are incised with imitation voussoirs. The west window is by far the richest (fig.55). It has two-strand interlace in the roll moulding of the arch, capitals in the form of huge masks with foliage issuing from the mouths, beaded interlace on the shafts, and bases in the form of upturned cushion capitals with concentric incisions on their faces.

Fig.53 The corner of the nave at Kilpeck showing Saxon-style long and short work

Fig.54 Panel at Kilpeck next to the south-west dragon's head

The South Doorway

The lavish south doorway is amongst the most richly carved of any parish church in England (fig.25).

The inner jambs comprise plain ashlar blocks on chamfered bases with hollow-chamfered and fine horizontal mouldings on the upper course. The latter are not continuous with the abaci, or upper part, of the adjacent capitals but are set just below their mid-point, a very unusual detail. Above the jambs the lintel is plain and yet it is enriched with vertical zigzags above the door itself. A significant detail is that the lower half of the tympanum is carved on the very same stone as the lintel, while two other stones (restored on the right) provide the top

of the tympanum (fig.5, *reproduced next page*), which is surrounded by twelve carved voussoirs—the wedge-shaped stones which form the arch.

The tympanum is carved with sparse foliage and grape clusters on striated stems that are beaded below the binding ties. The image is traditionally identified as the Tree of Life, or the tree of good and evil: 'And the Lord God planted a garden eastward in Eden; and there he put the man whom he had formed. And out of the ground made the Lord God to grow every tree that is pleasant to the sight, and good for food; the tree of life also in the midst of the garden, and the tree of knowledge of good and evil' (Genesis 2:8-9). Reference to Revelation (2:7) also seems to be intended: 'He that hath an ear, let him hear what the Spirit saith

Fig.55 The west window at kilpeck

Fig.5 The tympanum at Kilpeck

unto the churches; To him that overcometh will I give to eat of the tree of life, which is in the midst of the midst of the paradise of God.' Later, the tree of life is described as a fruit-bearing tree (Revelation 22.2). Keyser observes that reference to Christ as the True Vine may be intended (John 15:1).[15]

In the *Bestiary* one reads that 'The perindens is a tree found in India; the fruit of this tree is very sweet and pleasant, and doves delight in its fruit and live in the tree, feeding on it. The dragon, which is the enemy of doves, fears the tree, because of the shade in which the doves rest, and it can approach neither the tree nor its shadow. If the shadow of the tree falls to the west, the dragon flies to the east, and if the shadow is in the east, the dragon flies to the west. If it finds a dove outside the shadow of the tree, it kills it. The tree is God the Father, the shadow God the Son; in Gabriel's words to Mary "The Holy Ghost shall come upon thee, and the power of the Highest shall overshadow thee" [Luke 1:35]; the wisdom of the Lord is a heavenly fruit, that is, the dove or Holy Ghost. Watch therefore, O man, that you do not escape from eternal life after you have received the Holy Ghost, the spiritual dove of reason; and that, as a stranger to Father, Son and Holy Ghost, the dragon who is the devil does not kill you. Beware, O man, and dwell in the Catholic faith, and hold fast to the Catholic Church. Keep watch, as far as you are able, that you are not caught outside its doors and seized by that old serpent the devil and devoured, just as Judas, as soon as he left the Lord and his brother apostles, was at once devoured by a demon and perished.'[16]

Thus, on the Kilpeck doorway there is the threat of 'that old serpent the devil' on the lateral shafts, and while there are many dragons around the arch they do not harm the doves who are protected by the 'shadow of the tree' at the bottom of the inner right shaft.

The shafts that flank the plain, coursed door jambs are unusual in a number of respects. The appearance is of two shafts, a thicker inner one and a thinner one to its outside. However the base only 'supports' the main shaft and is flanked by the minor shaft. The cable necking of the capital spreads onto the upper extension of the outer shaft. Most unusually the capital, shafts and bases are not carved on separate stones but are fashioned from a single block on each side. All is richly carved.

On the main shaft of the left jamb are two knights entwined in stringy stems. The men are slim, have pointed faces and wear phrygian caps, striated hauberks and loose-fitting trousers held at the waist with a rope-like belt tied in a substantial knot (fig.36). The upper knight carries a cross over his right shoulder, while the lower knight holds a sword in a similar manner. To the outside the minor shaft is carved with two fleshy serpents, one biting the other's tail. They slither from top to bottom of the shaft amidst sparse stems. On the capital are roaring figures of a basilisk (a fabled reptile hatched from a cock's egg by a serpent and which could blast with both its breath and look) on the outside face, and a lion on the inside (fig.56) which claw feebly at each other. The two knights are especially fitting for the seigneurial church. The secular and sacred aspects of the knight's life are depicted respectively by the sword and the cross. Do we perhaps witness the perceived role in twelfth-century society of the patron, Hugh of Kilpeck, in the fight for good against the

Fig.56 The left hand capital to the south doorway at Kilpeck

entangling forces of evil, including the serpents on the minor shaft?[17] Evil is also represented on the left capital with the lion and the basilisk as referred to in Psalm 91:13 (Douay version) 'Though shalt tread upon the adder and the basilisk and trample under foot the lion and the dragon.'[18] This is the evil lion as described in the first epistle of Peter (5:8) 'your adversary the devil, as a roaring lion, walketh about seeking whom he may devour.' The serpents slither down the left minor shaft, but climb the shaft on the right. On the left they represent evil forces but on the right the interpretation is not so straightforward, and reference may be intended to Jesus' words to the disciples in sending them on their mission: 'be ye therefore wise as serpents, and harmless as doves' (Matthew, 10.16).

On the right of the doorway the capital is transformed into a huge human mask from which stylized foliage, of the same type as in the tympanum, issues from the mouth (fig.57). The capital has been variously interpreted. On the one hand, it has been seen as the preacher sending forth the fruitful Word of God, for the which the upper serpent on the minor shaft reaches, but does not obtain.[19] On the other hand, it may depict the temptation to eat the fruit of the tree of knowledge of good and evil.[20] The foliage and fruit on the capital is the same as on the tympanum but it is difficult to believe that the grotesque features of the mask could be equated with a priest. It is therefore more likely to represent evil and temptation associated with the serpent (Genesis 3:1-6).

On the main shaft on the right, there is thin, stylized, symmetrical foliage, except at the bottom where a pair of doves peck at each other's beaks. The moulded bases have beak spurs on the angle. Chip-carved, saltire crosses adorn the upper faces of both shafts' capitals above thin horizontal mouldings and a hollow chamfer. These extend well beyond the sides of the capitals to carry the outer order of the arch.

Unlike the majority of Romanesque doorways, at Kilpeck there is no direct correspondence between the jambs and the orders of the arch. There is a more-or-less direct relationship between the plain, inner door jambs and the inner moulded order of the arch, although there is the intervention of the plain section of stone to the side of the chevron on the lintel. The thick-thin juxtaposition of the shafts is reversed in the arch where a thin band of chevrons running at right-angles to the wall is placed above the thicker, inner shaft, while the wider roll-and-hollow moulding, encrusted with various creatures

Fig.57 The shafts and capital to the right of the doorway to Kilpeck

Figs.58 and 59 The springers of the arch to the south doorway at Kilpeck

and heads, is outside. At the springing of the arch the two elements are linked by means of a small, horizontal, winged dragon on the left and a grotesque head with a two-strand, interlaced body on the right (figs.58 & 59).

The struggle between good and evil continues in the arch where reference to the *Bestiary* is essential for an understanding of the carvings. To the left of the angel, God's messenger, at the apex of the middle order of the arch is the phoenix (fig.60) which is described in the *Bestiary* as follows: 'When it knows that the end of its life is approaching, it builds a chrysalis of frankincense and myrrh and other spices, and when it is about to expire it goes into the chrysalis and dies. From its flesh a worm emerges, which gradually grows up: in due course it grows wings and appears in the form of the previous bird. The bird teaches us by its example to believe in the Resurrection ...'[21]

Fig.60 The apex of the arch to the south doorway showing at the apex in the middle order, an angel and to his left a phoenix, with a dragon above the angel

47

*Fig.32 The arch of the south doorway at Kilpeck, showing voussoirs 1 to 6
and birds on the outer order*

Forces of evil are also present in the form of dragons and grotesque heads
on both the orders of the arch. However, the manner in which most of the
dragons are represented provides a sign of hope. The *Bestiary* relates that the
dragon is like the devil and that its 'strength is not in its teeth, but its tail.'[22] The
representation of the dragon on the doorway therefore suggests the weakening
or confusion of the devil. In the apex medallion (fig.60) the tip of the dragon's
tail is limp, as if it has lost its strength. In the lowest right medallion the tails
are entwined and the dragons snarl at each other. On the inner order the dragon
on voussoir No.2 turns to bite its own tail (fig.32). On voussoirs Nos.4 and 6
the dragons are devoured by grotesque masks (fig.32). The four dragons on
voussoir No.11 devour each others tails, while the dragon on voussoir No.12
bites its own tail (fig.33).

From left to right the carvings on the inner order of arch (fig.32) are:

1. A beak-head.

2. A dragon with gaping mouth and turned-back head, a beaded upper and
lower body with striated midriff, and a foliage-tipped tail that curls behind and
above the body.

3. A manticore (a human-headed lion) which 'has a threefold row of teeth meeting alternately: the face of a man, with gleaming, blood-red eyes, a lion's body: a tail like the sting of a scorpion, and a shrill voice which is so sibilant that it resembles the notes of flutes. It hankers after human flesh most ravenously ...'[23]

4. A heavily lined mask with two dragons' heads facing each other issuing from the mouth.

5. A beak-head with flattened, lined 'beak'.

6. A mask with dragons issuing from the mouth. Their bodies flank the mask and their heads are facing each other above.

7. A phoenix above stylized flames and a 'nest' composed of two-strand interlace (fig.60).

8. An angel carrying a scroll across his lower body (fig.60).

9. A mask with two sprigs of foliage hanging from the mouth (fig.60).

10. A classic beakhead with sharply pointed ears, a central tuft of curly hair, large almond-shaped eyes with drilled pupils, and a beak clasping the roll moulding (fig.60).

11. Four dragons' heads arranged in profile and devouring the next body in a clockwise direction (fig.33).

12. A single dragon in profile curling round to bite its own tail while clawing the top of its head (fig.33).

13. A dragon's head in profile (fig.33).

14. A variant on a beakhead with a long thin snout and flared nostrils and flattened striated cheeks.

The outer order of the south doorway starts on both sides with a large inverted dragon's head with huge bulbous eyes, heavily lined features and stylized foliage-like hair (fig.30). The large mouth, filled with sharp, shark-like teeth, points up to nine beaded medallions joined by grotesque masks which occupy the rest of the order. The first four on the left are occupied by birds in profile with crescent-shaped wings that curve emphatically above the bodies. The first three birds face west, the fourth towards the east. These

A detail from Fig.33 showing voussoirs 11, 12 and 13 on Kilpeck south doorway, together with medallions on the outer order

birds are difficult to interpret. Doves may be intended but, unlike the doves at the bottom of the main right shaft of the doorway, they have curved rather than straight wings. Therefore they may be cocks, an interpretation supported by comparison of the curved wings with the birds at St Peter's, Rowlstone (fig.179), where reference to the patron saint is direct (Matthew 26:34, 75). According to the *Bestiary*, the cock is feared by the lion.[24] Further, 'The devout to their prayers at cock-crow, and can read their books once more. When the cock crew thrice, the rock of the church was cleansed of the guilt he had incurred by his denial of Christ before cock-crow. Its song brings back hope to everyone, eases the pain of the sick, cools the fevered brow, brings back faith to those who have lapsed.'[25]

To the left of the central medallion of the curled dragon is a bird (fig.60) which may be interpreted as an eagle or an ibis. The *Bestiary* tells us that 'The eagle is so called because it is eagle-eyed. Its sight is so sharp that it can glide over the sea, beyond the ken of human eyes; from so great a height it can see the fish swimming in the sea. It will plunge down like a thunderbolt and seize its prey, and bring it ashore. When it grows old, its wings grow heavy and its eyes cloud over. Then it seeks out a fountain and flies up into the atmosphere of the sun; there its wings catch fire and the darkness of its eyes is burned away in the sun's rays. It falls into the fountain and dives under water three times: at once its wings are restored to their full strength and its eyes to their former brightness. So you, O man, whose clothes are old and the eyes of whose heart are darkened, should seek out the spiritual fountain of the Lord, and lift the eyes of your mind to God who is the fount of justice; and then you will renew your youth like the eagle.'[26] Meanwhile, the ibis 'purges its stomach with its beak. It uses serpents' eggs and the corpses of animals to make a very welcome meal for its young. For it is afraid to go into the water, because it does not know how to swim, so it walks up and down the shore, day and night, looking for dead fish or other bodies thrown up by the water. It is the image of carnally-minded men, who make their evil deeds their spiritual food, and nourish their pitiful souls with this food to their own destruction. But you, O Christian, reborn from water and the Holy Spirit, enter the spiritual waters of the mysteries of God, and eat the most wholesome foods, of which the Apostle tells us, saying "The fruit of the spirit is love, joy, peace, long-suffering, gentleness, goodness, faith and so on [Galatians 5:22]".'[27]

The other medallions contain two fish swimming in opposite directions and joined by a cord at their mouths (see detail of fig.33 on previous page)— the sign of Pisces where the fish swimming in opposite directions mark the opposites of good and evil in the earthly life; a two-legged monster with the head of a bird of prey (fig.33 detail); and lastly demi-figures of dragons facing each other.

The cornice has a beaded flat face, as in the chancel, but is more elaborate than the latter in having a hollow roll and a cable style roll below.

Corbels

Surrounding the apse, chancel and nave there is a series of elaborately carved corbels which have been little studied. The numbering system adopted here follows that established in *A short tour round the corbels*, a paper available in the church. It starts at the west end of the south wall of the nave and progresses in an anti-clockwise direction to the south corner of the west wall.

Are the corbels intended as decoration for the amusement of the viewer, or do they carry a similar message to the south doorway? Pevsner observed that 'the best have an irresistible comic-strip character',[28] while the anonymous writer of the *Guide to Kilpeck Church* calls attention to the 'very comical dog and rabbit.'[29] Both comments are quite valid; the corbels are surely meant to be 'irresistible'. However, they were not just for entertainment value but rather to educate the viewer. This is demonstrated, in the first place, by the two *Agnus Dei* on the axis of the apse (fig.87) and above the south doorway (fig.65). They mark the entry into the house of the Lord and provide external reference to the placement of the altar within the church. But what of the rest; is there a theme, or are there several themes, which can link human heads, half human and half animal heads, grotesque heads some of whom feast on human foes, rams, stags, fish, a female exhibitionist, a musician, dancers(?) and more?

That every corbel had one specific meaning is unlikely. But, it seems plausible to suggest that the rich variety of types reflects that variety of human experience, the struggle between good and evil as witnessed on the south doorway. There are real human beings (figs.62, 88, 101, 109, 111, 113, 117 & 118), including a knight on corbel No.75 (fig.109) on the north nave wall. The struggles of the figures (knights?) to attain heaven is seen in corbel No.7 on which they are fighting and on corbel No.10 (fig.66) where their arms become entwined like the knights are entwined in stems on the left shaft of the south doorway (fig.36). The human heads with leonine features may reflect emotion/behaviour (figs.63, 67 & 70), while the one with a bowl to his mouth (corbel No.64, fig.104) may represent gluttony. The stags (corbels Nos.65 & 74; fig.105), the fish (corbel No.70; fig.107), the horse (corbel No.72; fig.108), and the hound and hare (corbel No.33; fig.82) are appropriate to the lord of the manor's church with their reference to the hunt and fish ponds. In this connection it should be noted that there is a representation of a hunt on the south nave wall of the Romanesque church at Elkstone, Gloucestershire, where a knight, a hound and a stag are carved on three separate corbels. This does not preclude additional meaning for the Kilpeck corbels. Once again much is to be gleaned from the *Bestiary* to which reference is made for individual corbels in the list below.

In sum, the corbels reflect on aspects of life and serve as a mirror of morality. The evils of sexual promiscuity are blatantly displayed. Less forthright, but still clear, is the caution against the intoxicating effect of music. To balance this there are clear indications with interpretations of the dog, the hare, the stag and probably the ram, of the path of righteousness to be followed by the Christian in search of salvation.

South Nave

1. A large bird, with angled straight wing and long drooping tail, stands on and pecks the upper body of a smaller bird (fig.61). This type of composition is used in the *Bestiary* for three birds, the pelican, the quail and the kite. The pelican 'shows exceeding love for its young, if it has brought offspring into the world, when these grow up they strike their parents in the face. The parents strike back and kill them. After three days, their mother opens her own breast and side, and lies on her young, pouring all her blood over the dead bodies, and thus her love brings them back to life. So our Lord Jesus Christ, who is the author and originator of all creatures, begot us, and, when we did not exist, He made us. But we struck him in the face; as Isaiah said: "I have begotted sons

and raised then up, but they have despised me." Christ ascended the Cross and was struck in the side: blood and water came forth for our salvation, to give us eternal life.'[30] It is of little concern that the Kilpeck bird bears little resemblance to a pelican for nor do the *Bestiary* illustrations of them.

'Quails are so called from their cry; the Greeks call them "ortigias" because they were first seen on the island of ortygia. They travel at set times. When summer is over, they cross the sea, in a flock led by the "ortigometra". When a sparrow hawk sees the bird approaching

Fig.61 Corbel No.1

land, it tries to seize it, and for this reason the others do their best to protect it and to keep it safe from all dangers. Their favourite food is poisonous seeds, which is why the ancients forbade the eating of this bird. ... The quails also have their set time of arrival, because as soon as summer is over they fly across the sea. The heat of summer is the warmth of love, the winter frost the time of spiritual numbness. From his love of Christ and his neighbours, the just man crosses the sea of this world to the love of God, so he can always remain in its warmth. He who burns with love within wishes to avoid the frost of winter, that is, the storms and winds of unexpected temptation. ... The earth is earthly pleasure, the seas the danger of this world. The hawk is the devil, lurking in order to tempt us. Just as the hawk seizes the quail as it approaches land, so the devil uses those who approach earthly things out of greed as lackeys, because those who seek earthly things either for themselves or to fulfil the needs of their brethren will be seized by the hawk, that is the devil: they despise spiritual things in favour of earthly delights. So everyone should choose a good leader, who will avoid such dangers from the outset. There are two kinds of men, good and evil. Evil men are best at outward things. So just men choose evil as their leaders, and observe their actions closely. By paying attention they can detect their first leanings towards sin, and avoid them accordingly. This bird suffers, like man, from the falling sickness, because sin befalls the holy man just as much as the man of the world. He does not die whenever he sins, because the grace of repentance is not denied to him. So it is written: "For a just man falleth

seven times and riseth up again" [Proverbs 24.16]. For as often as just man sins, he strives to rise again.'[31]

The third bird, the kite, 'is weak both in strength and flight: its Latin name (*milvus*) comes from "*mollis avis*" (weak bird). It is nonetheless very rapacious and always attacks tame birds. The kite signifies, I think, the rapacious or proud man, as in the passage in the psalm: "The kite's home shall be in the fir-tree".'[32]

2. A human head, with bulging eyes and drilled pupils, channelled eyebrows, and cap-like hair combed to the sides from the centre (fig.62).

3. A humanoid lion's head with a mane and a curly cap of hair between the

Fig.62 Corbel No.2

Fig.63 (left) Corbel No.3; Fig.64 (centre) Corbel No.4;
Fig.65 (right) Corbel No.8

damaged ears on top of the head. The cheek bones are pronounced and to the sides of the damaged nose a pencil moustache loops below the cheeks. The eyes have drilled pupils and clearly defined lids which overlap at the outer corners. The wide mouth derives from a classical theatrical mask (fig.63).

4. Four symmetrically entwined scaly serpents with gaping mouths and flared lips, and (worn) large eyes without pupils (fig.64).

5 & **6** Missing.

7. Two wrestlers. Only the lower bodies are preserved. They wear flared striated trousers to just below the knee. The hand of the left wrestler can be made out grabbing the upper back of his opponent.

8. An *Agnus Dei* (Lamb of God) above the south doorway (fig.65).

9. Missing.

10. The main section of this corbel is completely defaced. There remain two male figures preserved from just above the waist down (fig.66). They are carved in profile like the wrestlers on corbel No.7 and wear similar flared trousers,

although those of the figure on the left are slightly shorter. The figure on the right also sports a sort of surcoat which is held tightly at the waist with a double rope-like belt and falls diagonally from the mid thigh. The arm towards the centre of the right figure preserves tightly fitting concentric rings of rope-like drapery. Most remarkably, the arms take on serpentine form. In each case the outer arm falls

Fig.66 Corbel No.10

Fig.67 (left) Corbel No.11 Fig.68 (centre) Corbel No.12;
Fig.69 (right) Corbel No.13

behind the thigh and then reappears between the legs with the hand on the ground like a third foot. There it is clasped by the figure's other hand at the end of the arm intertwined with its mate in the centre of the composition.

11. A close relation of the humanoid lion on corbel No.3 although this time with smaller, floppy ears and undrilled pupils (fig.67).

12. A grotesque head with large deeply hollowed ears on top of the head, large plain eyes, lion-like mane, lined face, a huge mouth with thick lips and shark-like teeth except in the middle where the fleshy tongue protrudes (fig.68).

13. Symmetrical two-strand interlace (fig.69).

(Buttress)

14. A humanoid lion head with rounded facial features (fig.70).

Fig.70 Corbel No.14

15. Three three-strand interlaced stems which terminate in fluted, pod-like leaves at the sides and corners of the corbel (fig.71).

16. A ram's head (fig.72). 'The rams [corbels Nos.16, 42, & 81] signify the Apostles or the princes of the Church. We read in Isaiah: "The rams of Nabaioth shall minister unto thee" [60:7], and in the Psalms: "Bring unto the Lord the offspring of rams." For the princes of the Church, like the leaders of the flock, shall lead the Christian people in the ways of the Lord. And we are told to offer the offspring of rams because such men are the result of the preaching of the Apostles, not

Fig.71 (left) Corbel No.15; Fig.72 (centre) Corbel No.16;
Fig.73 (right) Corbel No.17

some stranger who experiments with wicked teachings ... rams are like the Apostles because these animals have powerful foreheads and always over-throw whatever they strike. The Apostles did the same with their preaching, breaking down various superstitious and well-established idols with the heav-enly words. Elsewhere, however, the rams represent wicked rulers, as in Ezekial: "Arabia, and all the princes of Kedar, they occupied with thee in lambs, and rams, and goats" [27:21].'[33]

17. A leonine head with incised rings around the eyes, and flared, juicy lips and the upper lip doubling as a nostril (fig.73).

18 and **19**. Missing.

South Chancel

20. Missing.

21. A tapered animal head with large pointed ears and eyes shaped like verti-cally set semi-circles with curves towards the centre of an otherwise featureless face (fig.74). The mouth is damaged.

22. A rosette of three concentric rings of fluted petals (fig.75). Regarding this flower corbel 'As for man, his days are as grass: as a flower of the field, so he flour-isheth. For the wind passeth over it, and it is gone; and the place thereof shall know it no more. But the mercy of the Lord is from everlasting to everlasting upon them

Fig.74 Corbel No.21

Fig.75 (left) Corbel No.22; Fig.76 (centre) Flower of the same type from Aulnay-de-Saintoigne, western France; Fig.77 (right) Corbel No.23

that fear him, and his righteousness unto children's children' (Psalm 103:15-17). Similarly, 'For all flesh is as grass, and all the glory of man as the flower of grass. The grass withereth, and the flower thereof falleth away: But the word of the Lord endureth for ever. And this is the word by which the gospel is preached unto you' (1 Peter 1:24-25). A flower of the same type as this corbel is also seen on the north wall of the chancel at Aulnay-de-Saintonge, in western France (fig.76).

23. A bland, earless frog-like head with a huge, swollen tongue or other object in its mouth (fig.77).

24. Damaged hind quarters of a quadruped(?).

25 and **26**. Missing.

27. A pig's head with damaged snout. 'The pig (*porcus*) is a filthy beast (*spurcus*); it sucks up filth, wallows in mud, and smears itself with slime. ... Sows signify sinners, the unclean and heretics.'[34] 'The sow thinks on carnal things ...',[35] and is therefore suitable accompaniment at Kilpeck for the 'he-goat' (corbel No.87, fig.118) 'a stubborn, lascivious animal who is always eager to mate.'[36]

South stilted bay of apse

28. A female exhibitionist (Sheela-na-gig) with huge bald head, puny body and long arms which pass behind the legs to open the grossly enlarged vulva (fig.78). This represents low morals.

Fig.78 Corbel No.28

Fig.79 (left) Corbel No.29; Fig.80 (centre) Corbel No.30;
Fig.81 (right) Corbel No.32

29. A ball-shaped head with pointed ears and long snout which terminates in a beaked upper lip clasping a rod(?) in the mouth (fig.79). Lewis' lithograph of 1842 shows three-clawed feet in the lower corners of this corbel which are no longer extant.
(Buttress)

Apse
30. A muzzled bear's head with two small human heads poking out of the sides of the mouth (fig.80).
31. A bald, earless human head with cock-eyes, small mouth, goatee beard and upturned pencil moustache.
32. An ibex (fig.81). This corbel provides virtual proof of the connection between the Kilpeck corbels and the *Bestiary*. That it is carved upside down might be attributed to the error of the sculptor. However, reference to the *Bestiary* shows that it is intended to be represented in exactly this manner.[37] The ibex 'has two horns, which are so strong that if it falls from a high mountain down a precipice, its horns bear the whole weight of its body and it escapes unhurt. The beast represents those learned men who understand the harmony of the Old and New Testaments, and if anything

Fig.82 Corbel No.33

Fig.83 (top) Corbel No.35;
Fig.84 (centre) Corbel No.36;
Fig.85 (bottom) Corbel No.37

untoward happens to them, they are supported as if on two horns by all the good they have derived from reading the witness of the Old Testament and the Gospels.'[38]

33. A hound and a hare (fig.82), which look as if they have escaped from the Disney animation studio or the stage of the Muppet theatre, provide an early example of naturalistic observation more generally associated with the later twelfth century.[39] In the *Bestiary* the dog is described as having 'more understanding than any other beast. They also know their name and love their master.'[40] Dogs 'are like the preachers who by warnings and by righteous living turn aside the ambushes of the devil, lest he seize God's treasure, namely the souls of Christians, and carry it off. As the dog's tongue heals a wound when he licks it, so the wounds of sin are cleansed by the instruction of the priest when they are laid bare in confession' (Barber 1993, 76). The hare 'represents men who fear God, and who put their trust not in themselves but in the Creator.'[41]

34. A bald, earless head broken below the top lip but shown as pulling the mouth with both hands in Lewis' lithograph of 1842. This is associated with a warning against musical seduction, as indicated by Weir and Jerman,[42] who point to Isaiah 57:3-5, 'But draw near hither, ye sons of the sorceress, the seed of the adulterer and the whore. Against whom do ye sport yourselves? against whom make ye a wide mouth and draw out the tongue? are ye not children of transgression, a seed of falsehood, enflaming yourselves with idols under every green tree, slaying the children in the valleys under the clifts of the rocks?'

35. A beak head holding the arms, and biting the head of its human foe (fig.83).
(Buttress)

Fig.86 (left) Corbel No.38; Fig.87 (centre) Corbel No.39;
Fig.88 (right) Corbel No.40

36. Two fledgling birds biting a serpent, the head of which is on the left (fig.84).

37. A grotesque head with long snout and pointed, interlocking teeth (fig.85).

38. A humanoid lion head (fig.86).

39. An *Agnus Dei* on the main axis of the apse (fig.87) refers to the high altar within the apse.

40. A human head with short beard and hair, a pencil moustache, and gaping mouth (fig.88).

41. A striated grotesque head with flared lips (fig.89).

(Buttress)

42. A ram's head. (see reference to the *Bestiary* under corbel No.16)

43. A cat's(?) head (fig.90).

44. A fiddle player who seems to belong to the same family as the Sheela-na-gig on corbel No.28, and represents low morals (fig.91).

Fig.89 (left) Corbel No.41; Fig.90 (centre) Corbel No.43;
Fig.91 (right) Corbel No.44

Fig.92 (left) Corbel No.45; Fig.93 (centre) Corbel No.46;
Fig.94 (right) Corbel No.47

45. A pair of figures, with bald, earless, egg-shaped heads and tiny bodies clad in simple shifts, dancing(?) cheek-to-cheek (fig.92). The left figure (a male?) gropes the buttock of his (female?) partner but the advance is seemingly restrained by a firm grasp to the elbow to restrain further movement. The angle of the female's head also suggests resistance to a kiss, and is another corbel representing low morals and serves as a warning against musical seduction.

46. A pig's head biting a human figure whose large bald head extends to the right and thin legs to the left (fig.93).

47. A slim, bald, earless female(?) figure with head broken below the mouth, and turned away as if in horror or disgust (fig.94). She is dressed in a plain, tight-fitting tunic with a short, vertical cut just below the neck, and a ribbed, knee-length skirt gathered at the waist with a long belt the strands of which fall to the outside of the thighs. The legs are crossed and the body is carved on the diagonal of the corbel with the damaged left arm at the right side of the corbel and her right arm clinging to the top left. As if to accompany this warning about the dangers of lusty advances brought on by intoxicating music, the figure appears to recoil with legs crossed at the impending violation, quite unlike corbel No.28! (fig.78).

Corbel tables on the Romanesque churches of Saintonge, an area that exerted influence on the Herefordshire School, suggest an analagous interpretation. Musicians frequently appear, as on the main apse at Matha-Marestay, Charente-Maritime (fig.95), where a viol player is next to a 'dancing' cowering figure to the left with outstretched arms. On the other side of the viol player, a monster devours two souls, an immediate warning of the impending danger of the musical seduction. Similar warnings appear at Kilpeck in the form of

Fig.95 Corbel table at Matha-Marestay, Charente-Maritime , where a viol player is between a 'dancing' cowering figure to the left and, to the right, a monster devouring two souls, an immediate warning of the impending danger of the musical seduction.

human heads being eaten by beakheads and grotesque heads (corbels Nos.35, 50, 69 & 85), or in the shark-toothed grotesque on corbel No.37. (Buttress)

North stilted bay of apse
48. A striated grotesque head with long snout and broken mouth in which a few teeth are preserved (fig.96).
49. An alien-like, chinless, bald head with a long thick neck, pencil moustache, almond-shaped eyes, long thin snout-like nose, and a perfectly round mouth filled with a ball-like object (fig.97).
50. A beakhead with arms holding the human foe whose head is bitten (fig.98). This is seen as a warning against musical seduction.

*Fig.96 (left) Corbel No.48; Fig.97 (centre) Corbel No.49;
Fig.98 (right) Corbel No.50*

Fig.99 (top)
Corbel No.52;
Fig.100 (centre)
Corbel No.58;
Fig.101 (bottom)
Corbel No.61

North chancel

51. A damaged quadruped.

52. A squashed almost featureless human(?) head (fig.99).

53. A simple human head with ribbon-like strips of hair.

54. A simple bald, egg-shaped head, without ears. (Buttress)

55. A crudely executed head with ribbed, pill-box hat.

56. A simple human head with almond-shaped eyes, drooping moustache, and a strange triangular protrusion in the middle of the forehead.

57. A draped female(?) head with worried expression.

58. A cock-eyed, pear-shaped head (fig.100).

59. Missing.

North nave

60. Missing.

61. A human head with short curly hair and beard, small ears, beaded eyebrows, classical-theatrical-mask-like mouth, and pencil moustache growing to the sides of the nose (fig.101).

62. A large bird with the claw nearest the background raised (fig.102).

63. A sheep's(?) head with floppy ears and a strap across the mouth (fig.103).

64. An animal head biting the underside of an upturned bowl which it clasps in both hands (fig.104).

65. A stag running vertically up the corbel (fig.105). In the *Bestiary* the stag is the enemy of serpents: 'as soon as they feel the symptoms of illness, they entice snakes out of their holes with the breath of their noses, and overcoming their harmful poison, feed on them and are cured. ... Deer by nature like to change their homeland, and for this reason seek new pastures, helping each

Fig.102 (left) Corbel No.62; Fig.103 (centre) Corbel No.63;
Fig.104 (right) Corbel No.64

other on the journey. If they have to cross a great river or lake on the way, they place their heads on the hindquarters of the deer in front, and, in following each other, do not feel hindered by their weight. And if they come to a place where they might get dirty, they jump rapidly over it. Another peculiarity of their nature is that after they have eaten a snake, they hasten to a spring and, drinking of it, their grey hairs and all signs of old age vanish. The nature of the deer is like that of the members of Holy Church who leave this homeland (that is, the world) because they prefer the new pastures of heaven, and support each other on the way; those who are more perfect help their lesser brethren through their example and good works, and support them. If they find a place of sin, they spring over it at once, and if the devil enters their body after they have

Fig.105 (left) Corbel No.65; Fig.106 (centre) Corbel No.69;
Fig.107 (right) Corbel No.70

*Fig.108 (left) Corbel No.72; Fig.109 (centre) Corbel No.75;
Fig.110(right) Corbel No.78*

committed a sin, they hasten to Christ, the spring of truth, and confess, drinking in His commandments, and are renewed, laying aside their old guilt.'[43]
(Buttress)
66. A cat's(?) head with a human head in its mouth.
67. Three-strand interlaced stems growing from a central beaded binding tie at the lower centre of the corbel and sprouting now damaged leaves at the top.
68. A bearded, oval head with cat's ears.
69. A grotesque mask with concentric rings around the eyes and huge, flared lips devouring a human head (fig.106).
70. Two fish swimming up the corbel (fig.107). The skin of the fish on the left is scaly, that on the right is smooth. A single fish was used as a symbol of Christ by early Christians because the letters of his Greek name, Ichthys, formed an acronym of the initial letters for: Jesus Christ, Son of God, Saviour.
71. A human head with short beard, thin drooping moustache and a cap with concentric rings.
(Buttress)
72. A horse's head (fig.108).
73. A bird with back-turned head and crescent-shaped wing.
74. A stag running up the corbel. (See the *Bestiary* reference under corbel No.65)
75. A knight(?) with chain-mail cap and neatly groomed moustache and short beard (fig.109).
76. A damaged, plain, intertwined serpent.
77. Symmetrical beaded interlace.

Fig.111 (left) Corbel No.79; Fig.112 (centre) Corbel No.81;
Fig.113 (right) Corbel No.82

West nave

78. An elongated, pear-shaped head with hair like a judge's wig, a pronounced chin, and closely set eyes with drilled pupils (fig.110).

79. A male head with hair slickly groomed to the sides from a central parting, big eyes with drilled pupils, sharply arched eyebrows and a thin moustache growing to the sides of the face to just below the ears (fig.111).

80. Missing.

81. A ram's head (fig.112). (See reference to the *Bestiary* under corbel No.16)

82. A male head with moustache and beard (fig.113).

83. A grotesque head with broken mouth in which remains the outline of a devoured human head.

(Buttress)

84. A grotesque head.

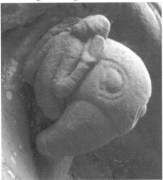

Fig.114 (left) and Fig.115 (centre) Corbel No.85;
Fig.116 (right) Corbel No.87

Fig.117 (top) Corbel No.88;
Fig.118 (bottom) Corbel No.89

85. A simple, plain beak head biting a human face whose upper body extends to the left and buttocks and legs to the right (figs.114 & 115).
86. Intertwined serpents.
87. A goat's head (fig.116). The he-goat is 'a stubborn, lascivious animal who is always eager to mate ...'[44]
88. A male head with short curly hair and beard, pencil moustache growing over the cheeks from the sides of the nose, and bulbous eyes (fig.117).
89. A close relation of the previous corbel (fig.118).

The Chancel Arch
The interior of the nave is quite plain except for the round-headed arch to the east which leads into the chancel. Originally the walls would have been painted; Lewis records having seen wall painting and paint on some of the sculpture when he visited the church in 1818, but it had gone when he returned in 1838.[45] On the chancel arch, as on the south doorway, there is not a direct correspondence between the orders of the jambs and the arch. The jambs have two orders, the inner, plain and of coursed ashlar, the outer, carved and monolithic except for the base and feet of the lower figures which are formed from a separate stone. The principles of design and fabrication are therefore the same as for the south doorway. The monoliths have three superposed figures, and are topped with a scalloped capital to the right and, to the left, a capital carved with foliage of the same type as on the tympanum and the right capital of the south doorway. Both capitals have cable necking which is plain on the left but beaded on the right.

As the appearance of the figures on the jamb of the chancel arch is quite different from the knights on the main left shaft of the south doorway (figs.36, 119-121), it has been suggested that the doorway and the chancel arch were not only carved by different sculptors but that the chancel arch was executed at a later date.[46] However, as noted above, the construction of the chancel arch shares many similar details with that of the south doorway, which suggests that they are contemporary. The figures may therefore look different in order to emphasise their different roles, religious on the one hand, secular on the other.

The middle figure on the left is immediately identifiable as St Peter because of the large key he carries over his right shoulder (fig.119). Of the others, those at the bottom carry a palm branch or aspergillum, the latter a brush for sprin-

kling holy water over the altar and people during the principal Mass on Sundays (fig.120). The remaining three figures are haloed, carry a book in their left hand, have egg-shaped heads, huge bulbous eyes, cap-like hair, tiny ears, drooping moustaches and generally glum expressions— features regularly encountered in the Herefordshire School. They are clad in tight, toga-like tunics and surcoats, have short arms, large hands and gigantic ankle bones. The lowest figures wear skull caps with concentric rings (fig.122). St Peter has a series of ribbon-like strands of hair brushed forward from the crown (fig.119), and the top left figure has a neatly groomed 'cap' combed over slightly from the left (fig.121). The middle and upper figures on the right have just a ring of hair around the side of the head. Boase has suggested that one of the figures may represent St Paul, another 'a figure with an uncertain emblem (probably an asperger [sic], appropriate to the entry to the chancel).'[47] Presumably Boase looked to a balding figure to

Fig.119 St Peter on the left jamb of the chancel arch, Kilpeck Church

Fig.120 Figure with aspergillium on the jamb of the chancel arch

identify St Paul, but both the top and middle figures on the right shaft are bald (fig.121). We may therefore be dealing with tonsured figures and consequently representations of church fathers. Boase may well be correct that the two lowest figures carry aspergillums. On the other hand, the carving could be of a palm branch in which case the figures may be martyr saints.

The tops of the capitals, which continue as string courses to carry the third order of the arch and onwards to the side walls, have hollow chamfers below finely detailed horizontal mouldings, as on the south doorway. On the upright section of stone there are incised semi-circles which are filled with three upright stylized leaves, except on the east face of the south jamb where they are plain. There are three orders to the arch. The inner order has a delicate angle roll moulding and a fine, raised, lozenged chevron with buttons in the interstices. The right-angled chevron of the second order matches that on the south doorway. The third order has a roll-and-hollow moulding plus flat chevron and a quirked square hood.

The chancel is quite plain as is the two-order arch that leads into the apse. The apse itself, on the other hand, is by far the most lavish part of the interior (fig.2). It is covered with a rib vault, as opposed to the wood roofs in the chancel and nave. The ribs are richly carved with two different types of lozenged chevron, and converge on a central boss carved with four cats' masks

Fig.121 Upper figure on the left jamb of the chancel arch

Fig.122 Figure with aspergillium(?) on the jamb of the chancel arch

69

biting the ribs (fig.113). The ribs are 'supported' on narrow pilasters with various multi-scalloped capitals and angle shafts on beak-spur bases (fig.4). The heads of the windows, like the ribs, are adorned with chevron, and there are nook shafts with scalloped capitals.

CHAPTER 5

Shobdon

Introduction

The *Chronicle of Wigmore Abbey* recounts that Hugh de Mortimer 'chose a wise, prudent and conscientious man named Oliver de Merlimond, and made him chief steward of all his land and manager of all his property.' On his appointment as steward Hugh de Mortimer gave Oliver the vill of Shobdon. 'At that time there was no church at Shobdon, but only a chapel of Saint Juliana, made of wood, subject to the church of Aymestry. Oliver was therefore most concerned to have erected a new church in Shobdon.' After Oliver had undertaken the construction of the church, he 'had the great wish to undertake a pilgrimage to St James (Santiago de Compostella) and entrusted to a knight, Bernard, all the responsibility for the work with the necessary funds.' On his return from Santiago de Compostella Oliver stayed at the Abbey of St Victor in Paris. 'And when his church was quite complete, he most humbly begged lord Robert of Bethune, Bishop of Hereford ... to consecrate his church at Shobdon.' Subsequently, Oliver wrote to the abbot of St Victor in Paris 'begging him to send two or three canons. Since the letter was sealed unofficially, however, the abbot refused and only when Oliver had sent a joint letter with Bishop Robert did the abbot agree and in due course two canons were installed in a very fine house near the church.'[1]

Unfortunately the *Wigmore Chronicle* does not give dates for these events. Robert de Bethune was bishop of Hereford between 1131 and 1148. In 1143, during the civil war, Miles, Earl of Hereford, a supporter of Matilda, demanded large sums from the church to pay his troops. When Bishop Robert refused to pay, Miles invaded his lands, and the bishop accepted Oliver de Merlimond's invitation to live at Shobdon. Bishop Robert returned to Hereford after Earl Miles was killed in a hunting accident on Christmas Day 1143. It is most likely that

*Fig.123 (top) The south doorway arch at Shobdon Church (after Lewis),
compared with the south transept doorway at Aulnay-de-Saintogne,
Fig.124 (below)*

Shobdon Church was completed and consecrated soon after Robert de Bethune became Bishop of Hereford in 1131, which would place Oliver de Merlimond's pilgrimage some time between 1125 and 1130.[2] Bernard probably prepared for the work but did not begin construction until Oliver returned. Oliver's return via Paris indicates that he took the overland route through western France, notably through Poitou and Saintonge where doorways are commonly carved with radiating figurated voussoirs as on the north and south doorways at Shobdon. The south transept doorway at Aulnay-de-Saintonge has been cited in relation to the south (right) doorway at Shobdon (figs.123 & 124), and the west doorway at Maillezais, Vendée, paralleled with the Shobdon north (left) doorway.[3] The Maillezais portal has already been cited in connection with the superposed knights on the left shaft of the Kilpeck south doorway, but the figures on the shaft at Maillezais are even closer to Shobdon (figs.37 & 137). Also common in Aquitaine, but relatively rare elsewhere, are carved abaci which occur at Shobdon and on the south transept portal at Aulnay-de-Saintonge. The inclusion of tympana in the Shobdon doorways, however, is quite alien to western French practice and, like Kilpeck, must be seen within the local tradition.

The Romanesque church of Shobdon was demolished in 1752 by Lord Bateman and was replaced by the present 'gem of our "Rococo Gothic"' built to plans sent from London in 1751.[4] The chancel arch and north and south doorways from the old church were re-erected in the park about a quarter of a mile to the north of the church as a folly with the addition of gables, pinnacles and crockets according to the fashion of the day. Most of the detail of the arches is now lost but study of the once magnificent sculpture is facilitated by Lewis' lithographs of 1852 and the plaster casts which were photographed before their destruction in the 1936 fire at the Crystal Palace. The Romanesque font, however, is still in the church. In 1998 work was carried out under the directions of S.T. Walker & Partners to stabilise the structure of the arches and to arrest further flaking of the stones.

Description and Sources

Two tympana are preserved, on the left the Harrowing of Hell (fig.125), and, on the right, Christ in an oval mandorla supported by four angels (figs.126 & 131). When fitted in the doorways the tympana would have extended below the abaci which carry the orders of the enclosing arches in a manner analogous to the south doorway at Kilpeck. In the Harrowing of Hell the tall figure of Christ is dressed in a knee-

Fig.125 Harrowing of Hell tympanum, Shobdon (after Lewis)

Fig.126 Ascension/Christ in Majesty tympanum, Shobdon (after Lewis)

length tunic. He moves from the right across the centre of the tympanum and with His right hand thrusts a long staff with a cross at the top into the mouth of the devil, whilst with His left hand He pulls the tiny figure of Adam from hell. Behind Christ stand two female figures, the taller one, probably Eve, is next to Christ, the shorter one is to the outside. On the left, standing before the cross-headed staff, is a tall, bearded figure who has been identified as possibly David or Solomon,[5] but St John the Baptist seems like a better candidate, by association with the font at Eardisley (see Chapter 8). To the outside there is a shorter, cowled(?) figure. The Harrowing of Hell tympanum was probably placed over the north doorway as at Beckford, Worcestershire, and Quenington, Gloucestershire,[6] and thus the Christ and angels would have been above the south doorway as, locally, at Rowlstone (fig.178).

Fig.127 Left arch, Shobdon, first and second pillars (after Lewis)

The left arch has two orders which are carried on richly carved capitals, shafts and bases (fig.123). The inner order has fine interlaced patterns carved on individual voussoirs and is framed by three rows of beads, a version of the double row of beads that frame the tympana at Dymock and Kempley, Gloucestershire. The second order follows the same principle of one motif carved on each voussoir but here there are fantastic quadrupeds in violently twisted poses. The third order is carved with four serpents with gaping mouths and knotted bodies like the jambs of the Kilpeck south doorway (figs.25 & 123).

Both capitals of the outer order (Lewis' first and fourth pillars) have three standing figures separated by stylized trees (figs.128 & 129). Five of the figures cup their cheeks with their right hand and hold their left hand across the waist and appear to be in mourning. The right figure of the outer right capital has arms folded across the waist and shoulders hunched as if in disapproval or stubbornness. The mourning figures have been identified as the five foolish virgins and are attended by the Lord as guard at the door (Matthew 25:1-13).[7] They serve as a

warning to prepare for entry in heaven. On the inner left capital (the second pillar) there are two

Fig.128 Left arch, Shobdon, third and fourth pillars (after Lewis)

branches of foliage arranged like the head of a crozier, while on the right capital (third pillar) there is a knotted, scaly serpent entwined in thin stems, a close relative of the serpents on corbel No.4 at Kilpeck (fig.64). The centre and right (third and fourth) shafts are both carved with elaborate single-strand interlace, and there is beaded interlace on the outer (first) shaft on the left side. The inner left shaft has five pairs of superposed male figures dressed in ribbed garments with calf-length trousers who grapple with entwining stems like the knights on the left shaft of the Kilpeck south doorway struggling to escape from the evil forces represented by the entangling vegetation (figs.36 & 127). They are secular figures, but unlike the Kilpeck sword bearer they do not carry the attributes of a knight. Evil forces are also present in the form of an inverted grotesque mask on the base beneath the figures, and an entwined serpent on the outer base. Similarly, on the right side, two serpents issue from an inverted grotesque mask on the outer base. The abaci are adorned with a variety of foliage. The outer order is

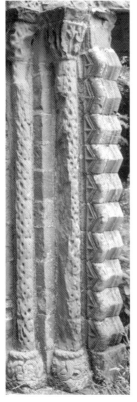

Fig.129 Right jamb of the left arch of Shobdon, as it survives today

Fig.130 Right arch, Shobdon (after Lewis)

carried on a jamb without a capital or base and is carved with a double row of 90-degree chevron to either side of a hollow roll. There are spears on the inner triangles of the chevron (fig.129).

The right arch, from the original south doorway, enclosed the Christ and angels tympanum, and like the north doorway has three orders (fig.130). On the inner order the carving is confined to one motif for each voussoir. There are birds and lions(?) set in frenzied patterns often with beaded interlace. The details are somewhat differently depicted in the plaster cast for no apparent reason. A single row of beads frames the order as on the tympanum at Pauntley, Gloucestershire (fig.24). The second order is carved with figurated radiating voussoirs. The following description is based on Lewis' lithograph enhanced with reference to the photographs of the plaster cast (fig.131)—parenthetic observations are included where the lithograph and cast are different. At bottom left, voussoir No.1, is an Agnus Dei. Voussoir No.2 has a lion with a long tail passing between its hind legs and over its body to terminate in a trefoil above the body (this is repeated as voussoir No.3 in the cast); No.3, a lion; No.4, a lion with back-turned head to bite the middle of its long tail; No.5, a bull (lion in the cast); Nos.6 & 7, lions (No.8 in the cast is a lioness); No.8, two wrestlers like those on Kilpeck corbel No.7; No.9, two standing figures clad in ankle-length robes (the cast shows them holding their arms before their chests; the left figure holds the right wrist with the left hand, and the right figure *vice versa*); No.10 as voussoir No.9 except that the left figure clasps his hands in prayer while the right figure folds his hands in front of his chest; No.11, two

Fig.131 Plaster cast of right arch, Shobdon, which was destroyed in the Crystal Palace fire in 1936. The tympanum is preserved in the Victoria and Albert Museum

standing figures with robes to the ground (above the ankles in the cast) and arms folded firmly across the chest (in the cast each figures holds the left arm above the head and clasps the left elbow with the right hand; No.12, a siren; No.13, the cast shows a frontal figure with thin waist and billowing, full-length skirt, and hands held in prayer; No.14, a standing angel; No.15, a pair of standing figures dressed in tunics which fall just below the knee. They fold their arms tightly across the chest (the cast depicts a mirror image of voussoir No.11); No.16, two standing figures as on voussoir No.15 (in the cast they cross their hands in front of the chest); No.17, two wrestlers; No.18, a bull; Nos.19 & 20, each with two fish like Kilpeck corbel No.70 (fig.107); No.21, a stag as on two of the Kilpeck corbels (fig.105); No.22, a goat(?); No.23, a stag; No.24, a lion.

The third order of the arch is terminated with serpents' heads with gaping mouths and three-strand, ribbon-like interlaced bodies with a thread running through them. As on the north doorway it is carried on chevron jambs.

Fig.132 (top) First and second pillars,
Fig.133 (bottom) Third and fourth
pillars of the left arch, Shobdon
(after Lewis)

The supporting columns are completely carved. On the inner left abacus (first pillar) (fig.132) and both right abaci (fig.133) there are sparsely foliated stems with binding ties. On the outer left abacus are four pairs of birds whose bodies cross as they peck each other's wings. The inner left capital has foliated scrolls in the form of two crozier heads. The outer left capital has a dragon facing outwards with the leg closest to the background raised in the manner of the lion and the basilisk on the left capital of the Kilpeck south doorway (fig.56), and a long, scaly body entwined in a thin stem. The inner right capital has eight standing figures who wear long robes. The outer right capital is carved with a pair of lion-like quadrupeds who snarl and claw at each other, and whose features compare with the creatures on the left capital of the Kilpeck south doorway and the panel behind the dragon's head at the south-west corner of the nave at Kilpeck (figs.54 & 56). All the capitals have beaded necking. The shafts all have interlace decoration but the left and right sides are different. Single-strand interlace is used on the left (Lewis' first and second pillars) while on the right (Lewis' third and fourth pillars) there is beaded inter-lace with sparse foliage and binding ties. Moulded bases are used on the right, while on the left the outer base is difficult to decipher, and the inner base has two-strand interlace.

The tympanum has a huge central enthroned Christ with His right hand raised in blessing and the left holding the top of a huge closed book which he balances on His left thigh (figs.126 & 131). He appears to be seated although there is no sign of a throne, and His knees are splayed to the extreme and feet held fairly close together, as in the capital from the east arch of the presbytery at Hereford Cathedral (fig.134). He has a thin waist with horizontally ribbed draperies and an overgarment with regular vertical folds which covers the thighs and knees to fall in a V-shape between the legs. An undergarment with repetitive, rib-like folds falls to His feet. He is surrounded with a beaded, oval mandorla, which is grasped by four

Fig.134 Capital from east arch of the presbytery, Hereford Cathedral, showing Christ seated in a similar position to that on the tympanum at Shobdon

elongated angels with arms held high above their heads. The lower angels swoop from the middle of the sides of the tympanum, while the upper angels swoop up from the middle and where their feet meet. Like Christ they have thin waists with ribbed, horizontal folds to the garments which are comparable to those on the hauberks of the Kilpeck knights (fig.36). The south tympanum may be intended as an Ascension to balance the Descent into Hell on the north tympanum. This is the usual representation of the Ascension in Byzantine art.[8] Zarnecki makes a close comparison with an ivory in the National Museum in Munich.[9] He explains the link with Shobdon through Carolingian art especially the Utrecht Psalter illustration to Psalm VIII on folio 4v.[10] This manuscript was copied at Canterbury around the year 1000 in the Harley Psalter.[11] The tympanum of the south doorway at Malmesbury Abbey, on which there is a seated Christ in a mandorla flanked by two angels, has also been interpreted as an Ascension.[12] However, there is an ambiguity, for in the Anglo-Saxon boxwood casket in the Cleveland Museum of Art,[13] a seated Christ in a mandorla flanked by four angels is on the lid while below on the side is the

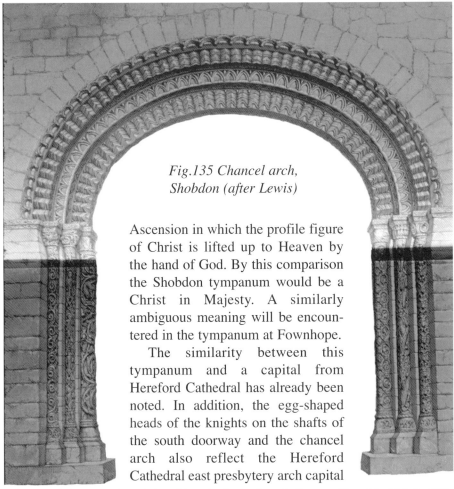

*Fig.135 Chancel arch,
Shobdon (after Lewis)*

Ascension in which the profile figure of Christ is lifted up to Heaven by the hand of God. By this comparison the Shobdon tympanum would be a Christ in Majesty. A similarly ambiguous meaning will be encountered in the tympanum at Fownhope.

The similarity between this tympanum and a capital from Hereford Cathedral has already been noted. In addition, the egg-shaped heads of the knights on the shafts of the south doorway and the chancel arch also reflect the Hereford Cathedral east presbytery arch capital

with the flying angel and the Kilpeck chancel arch figures (figs.11, 121-2, 127, 137). A further indication of the role of Hereford Cathedral in the formative stages of the Herefordshire School may come from the sculpture on the imposts of the south doorway of St Andrew's, Bridge Sollers. Domesday (2.48) records that Bridge Sollers was held by the bishop of Hereford. Construction of the church is not documented but we may suppose some episcopal role in it. The left impost of the Bridge Sollers doorway has a shallow carving of a feline head with two dragon's heads spewing from the mouth to either side of the head similar to the base of the third column of the left arch at Shobdon (fig.128). The head of the dragon on the left with gaping mouth and huge eye without a pupil compares favourably with the dragon on the capital of the same Shobdon column. On the right impost a single dragon with curled, beaded tail like the left capital of Kilpeck south doorway and wings and an upper body like voussoir No.12 on Kilpeck south doorway (figs.33 & 56), but the foliage trail on the abacus is a more compact version of the third and fourth capitals of the Shobdon left arch (fig.128). The Bridge Sollers sculpture is not of the same high quality as Shobdon and Kilpeck and probably represents the work of a lesser hand, possibly an apprentice from the cathedral workshop.

The chancel arch has three orders with geometric ornament in the arch but rich figurated carvings on the monolithic columns (fig.135) The inner order of the arch has chevron which meets to form lozenges filled with crosses in the soffit. Order two has a series of radiating, moulded pointed arches with triangular wedges in the spandrels. Order three has 90-degree chevron. There is a row of moulded semi-circles on the hood. The inner left shaft (first pillar) is covered with symmetrical foliage which curls in crozier-like heads (fig.136). On the capital a dragon writhes in entwining thread. On the abaci there are demi-figures identified as canons by Hamer. The second shaft has five pairs of superposed male figures exactly as on the inner shaft of the north doorway (fig.137). On the capital there are two crozier-like foliage scrolls while on the base there is a closely plaited knot. Shaft No.3 on the left has a inhabited scroll which spirals around to form five loosely defined medallions

Fig.136 (top) First pillar and Fig.137 (bottom) Second Pillar of the chancel arch at Shobdon (after Lewis)

Fig.138 Third pillar of the chancel arch at Shobdon (after Lewis)

(figs.138 & 139). At the top are two standing figures clad in long robes. The one on the left carries a book before his chest with his left hand and holds the key with his right hand to identify him as St Peter. The right figure also holds a book in the same manner as St Peter, while in his right hand he holds a Y-shaped branch. They are flanked by two birds and there are four more birds in the 'spandrels' of the spiral. In the second spiral there is a standing, robed figure holding a book(?) and a smaller version of the Y-shaped branch. To the figure's right one bird pecks at another's head as they both stand on a fish which swims up-column. On the other side of the figure there are two more birds and a further two inhabit the 'spandrel' between the spiral. The pecking birds, probably doves, were met at the bottom of the right shaft of the south doorway at Kilpeck, while on Kilpeck corbel No.1 several possible interpretations of the bird life were suggested with reference to the *Bestiary*. This source also offers two explanations for the appearance of a fish with the birds at Shobdon. In the *Bestiary* both the eagle and the osprey are depicted catching a fish in their claws. The eagle was introduced in connection with Kilpeck corbel No.1. The osprey, so the text of the *Bestiary* relates, is 'smaller than an eagle but larger than a hawk.' It has one foot 'equipped with talons, open and ready to seize prey, while the other is closed and peaceful, suited only to swimming. Like the eagle they spot fish with keen eyesight and then dive into the water and use their swimming foot to control their movement, seizing their prey with their talons, in which they carry it off. So the ancient enemy of mankind sees with his sharp intellect whatever we do in the turbulent waves of this world; and while he seems to approach us on a

Fig.139 Third pillar of the chancel arch at Shobdon (after Lewis)

peaceful footing through success in worldly things, he nonetheless seizes and destroys our soul with grasping talons, bloody with prey.'

In the next 'medallion' down there is the pecking bird motif with a lion above and to the right, and a stag in the outside to the right. The lion bows its head towards the bird in the manner of *Bestiary* depictions of the lion's fear of the cock. To the left there is a lion with head turned *en face* and the same motif is repeated immediately below. In spiral No.4 a bird pecks the mouth of a stag who runs up the shaft. To the left, below the stag, is another bird. To the right above the bird, is a fish. Two more birds occupy the lower spandrels and a final scroll with two birds occupies the middle ring. The fish held in the claws of a bird on the right of the second medallion has been explained with reference to the *Bestiary* illustrations of the eagle and the osprey. The inclusion of a second fish suggests adaptation from the *Bestiary* depiction of the fish in which they are shown intermingled with other creatures.

Fig.140 Fourth pillar of the chancel arch at Shobdon (after Lewis)

Fig.141 Fourth pillar of the chancel arch at Shobdon (after Lewis)

On the right of the chancel arch the inner shaft (fourth pillar) is covered with ten rows of beaded medallions joined by grotesque masks, in the manner of the outer order of Kilpeck south doorway, and filled with lions, birds, serpents, interlaced knots and a griffin (figs.140 & 141). Lewis' lithograph shows the top row and the two lateral medallions in the second row and the left medallion of the fifth row all worn away. The capital is also completely worn. But the base has three rows of different interlace. The birds are closely related to those in the four left medallions of the Kilpeck south doorway although,

*Fig.142 (top) Fifth pillar and
Fig.143 (bottom) base of fifth pillar,
base of third pillar and capital and
shaft of sixth pillar of the chancel
arch at Shobdon (after Lewis)*

unlike them, four of the Shobdon
birds turn their heads back to preen.
In the fourth row the central medallion is filled with a variant of the
pecking-bird motif encountered on
Kilpeck corbel No.1 (fig.61). It has
been suggested that this motif may
have been inspired by Anglo-Saxon
metalwork as in the famous purse
lid from the Sutton Hoo, Suffolk,
ship burial, *c*.625.[14] The second
column (fifth pillar) has a capital
with seven standing, robed figures
and an abacus with birds on the flat
and the chamfered face worn off to
the right (figs.142 & 143). There is
cable necking then four pairs of
dragons climbing up the shafts
amidst fine intertwined stems. The
outer shaft (sixth pillar) has a paired
foliated-crozier capital and cable
necking (fig.143). On the shaft are
eleven paired oval medallions
joined by grotesque masks ad filled
with doves whose heads pass under
the medallion to meet looking down
in the interstices (fig.144). There are
two types of interlaced foliage on
the base.

As at Kilpeck, there are indications in the Shobdon sculpture of
reference to pre-Conquest forms,
not least in the sumptuous arts. The
great variety of interlace, and especially the very fine type on the inner
order of the left arch, recalls the rich
decoration of insular manuscripts
like the Lindisfarne Gospels (698-
721).[15] The same tradition explains

the proliferation of fine interlacing lines surrounding the
dragons at Shobdon. This tradition was carried through into
the the twelfth century in Irish
manuscripts, metalwork, and
the 'ornamental' crosses.[16]
Similarly in Wales a wide
variety of interlace appears on
the sculptured crosses traditionally dated to the tenth and
eleventh centuries.[17] For the
Shobdon shafts the decoration
on the angle shafts of the lower
section of the cross at
Llandough, Glamorganshire, is
particularly close (fig.29).
Furthermore, on the stem of the
early tenth-century(?) Conbelin
Stone, preserved in the
museum at Margam Abbey,
there are two figures with large
egg-shaped heads, of which the
one on the left is remarkably
close to the Shobdon shaft figures.

*Fig.144 Sixth pillar of the chancel arch at
Shobdon (after Lewis)*

The Font

The Romanesque font is preserved in the church. It has a damaged, plain bowl
set on a thick stem on which are carved 'four sinister lions'.[18] On the one hand,
a sinister meaning is supported with reference to the late twelfth-century font
at St Mary's, Stafford, which also has lions carved on the stem.[19] An accompa-
nying inscription reads: DISCRETUS NON ES SI NON FUGIS ECCE
LEONIS (You are not wise if you do not flee from the lions). On the other hand,
the *Bestiary* informs us that 'when the lioness brings forth her cubs, they come
into the world dead. She watches over them for three days, until on the third
day the father comes, blows in their faces, and awakens them to life. In the
same way the Almighty Father awoke our Lord Jesus Christ from the dead on
the third day.'[20] Thus the lions provide a link between the sacraments of
Eucharist and Baptism also marked by the chalice shape of the font.[21]

Conclusion

Oliver de Merlimond's pilgrimage to Santiago de Compostella explains the appearance of western French motifs at Shobdon. Zarnecki suggested that a sculptor may have accompanied Oliver to make sketches *en route*. Local geometrical elements do not require special explanation but the fine interlace and animal interlace, whether from manuscripts or metalwork, display a link with a pre-Conquest tradition of art of the very highest order, and imbue the work at Shobdon with a shrine-like richness. At the same time the incorporation of the interlace may be read as an assimilation of a Welsh tradition within the more cosmopolitan context of the new Norman rulers. As at Kilpeck, there is reference to the most prestigious contemporary projects: the inhabited medallions on the fourth pillar of the chancel arch relate to Reading Abbey.[22] Once again we are dealing with a very ambitious patron who wished to be ranked with royalty and the top ecclesiastical rulers of the day. References to the *Bestiary* in the sculpture may be seen as a sign of learning in the patron, and this view is substantiated by the complexity of the Christ in Majesty/Ascension iconography. It may indeed indicate that Oliver de Merlimond was directly involved in the creation of the iconographic programme. Oliver was a man of letters. He was entrusted with the education of Hugh de Mortimer's son which suggests at the very least that his intellect was respected by his master. He was closely associated with Robert de Bethune, Bishop of Hereford, who gave up his career as a schoolmaster to study under William de Champeaux at St Victor in Paris, and Anselm of Laon, William's master.[23] This provides the introduction for Oliver to the intellectual ambiance of St Victor in Paris. The tradition of learning was instilled in the family. Oliver's son, Odo, was given the benefice of the church at Aymestry by Hugh de Mortimer, while his other son, Simon, became a canon and later abbot of Wigmore.[24]

CHAPTER 6

Sculpture connected with Hugh de Mortimer of Wigmore, and Oliver de Merlimond

The account in the *Chronicle of Wigmore Abbey* of Oliver de Merlimond's appointment as chief steward to Hugh de Mortimer with responsibility for all the Mortimer lands and the management of the property, invites investigation of other churches in which de Merlimond may have had a hand bearing in mind his role at Shobdon. The churches are at Aston and Brinsop in Herefordshire; Rock and Ribbesford in Worcestershire; and at Alveley in Shropshire. In none of these cases is there precise documentation as there was for the foundation of Shobdon, so that it is largely through consideration of the sculpture, its style and iconography, by which the links with Oliver de Merlimond and Hugh de Mortimer may be established.

ASTON, St Giles
Domesday (9.4) records Aston as part of the land of Ralph de Mortimer. The tympanum of the north doorway of St Giles' church has been considered as the first work of the Aston Master who later worked at Shobdon, Kilpeck and else-where.[1] The relative dating of Aston in relation to Shobdon is likely to remain a moot point but there can be no doubt as to the close similarity between the sculpture in the two places.

St Giles, Aston, comprises a rectangular Romanesque nave and square-ended chancel, the east end of which was rebuilt in the late thirteenth century (fig.145). The nave preserves its original doorways. The south one is plain and has a massive lintel and a single order arch with unmoulded voussoirs which frame a tympanum composed of two rows of three stones. This composite form of tympanum is frequently found in Herefordshire Romanesque churches as in the south doorway at Edvin Loach, the south and west doorways at Letton, the west doorway at Castle Frome, and the south doorway at Hampton Bishop.[2]

Fig.145 Church of St Giles, Aston

The north doorway, in this case probably the main entrance, has a carved tympanum and imposts, a single-order, chevroned arch and plain jambs (fig.146). In the centre of the tympanum is a medallion carved with saltire crosses and filled with the *Agnus Dei* which is intended to 'remind the faithful that they are entering the holy house of the Saviour.'[3] A griffin, to the left, as on the fourth pillar of the chancel arch at Shobdon, and a bull, to the right, couch the medallion in their wings. Below there is a row of triple billet ornament. The central section of the tympanum is surrounded with a frieze-like frame carved with two quadrupeds on each side. On the right and upper left

Fig.146 Tympanum of north doorway, Aston. Note the possible link between the beast on the left of the tympanum with that on a capital from Hereford Cathedral, opposite (fig.147)

88

their heads are carved in profile but on the lower left the head is turned to the audience like the lions on the Shobdon font. At the top of the tympanum there are two asymmetrical foliage sprays. The one on the right issues from the mouth of the beast. In the centre a large bird alights on the back of a smaller bird and pecks its head, exactly as on the fourth pillar of the Shobdon chancel arch (figs.140 & 146). The tympanum is framed with a roll moulding, a shallow version of the same motif on the south doorway at Kilpeck (figs.5 & 146). The left impost is carved with three dragons. On the upper section the head faces right and the beaded body is interlaced to the left where its tail is bitten by the second dragon. This creature's double outlined body curls onto the chamfered section of the impost, where its tail is bitten by the third dragon. This one has a beaded body, both ends of which terminate in a head. The motif of the inter-lacing dragons is allied to the outer order of both the left and right arches (north and south doorways) at Shobdon (fig.130). The details of the bodies are different in each case but in terms of technique the flat, ribbon-like appearance of the Aston dragons relates most closely to the right arch at Shobdon. The right impost of the Aston doorway has a foliage trail with hollowed, trefoil leaves. The enclosing arch has a channelled chevron with triangular wedges under-neath which is loosely paralleled on the south doorway at Moccas.[4] The tympanum, arch and imposts are carved in three different coloured sand-stones—grey for the tympanum, red for the arch, and yellow for the imposts. Presumably the intention was for this to be seen and therefore the sculptures would not have been painted.

A number of tympana in the area are carved with the *Agnus Dei* but none is stylistically close to Aston.[5] A link with Hereford Cathedral is suggested between the quadruped on the left of the Aston tympanum with the lion of the capital from the Hereford Cathedral east presbytery arch, with the elongated body and head turned *en face* with round, staring eyes (figs.146 & 147). This may indicate that the Aston Master received his training in the Hereford Cathedral workshop.

Fig.147 Samson/David and the lion capital from east presbytery arch, Hereford Cathedral

The pecking bird motif repeats the Shobdon version of the theme where the possibility of an Anglo-Saxon source was suggested. Pre-Conquest ancestry may also account for the double outline of the dragons' bodies as on the cross shaft at Desborough,

Northants.,[6] or on a cross shaft at Penally, Glamorganshire.

As at Kilpeck and Shobdon there are indications at Aston of more exotic connections for the sculpture. The animal frieze around the tympanum has been compared with one from Santa Margherita at Como preserved in the Museo Civico at Como.[7]

The stoup at Aston is also a product of the Aston Master (figs.148). The carving is now upside down suggesting that it is not serving its original function. It may have been a cross base. The lion's

Fig.148 The stoup at Aston, carved by the Aston Master

head is in profile and has a large eye and flared lips as on the south portal at Kilpeck. It turns back its head and has a two-strand stem spewing from its mouth which curls over its head and issues trefoil foliage as on the panels at the corners of the Kilpeck nave and the Hereford Cathedral nave arcade capitals (figs.6 & 7). The lion is pursued by a dragon whose body is double outlined as on the left impost of the Aston north doorway.

The close similarities between the sculpture at Aston and Shobdon, in connection with the Mortimer ownership of the land, make likely the attribution to Hugh de Mortimer through the office of Oliver de Merlimond.

Like Kilpeck and Shobdon the church at Aston was accompanied by a castle which was located about 140 yards to the north-east of the church[8] although it may not have been constructed of stone.[9]

ROCK, Worcestershire, St Peter

The documentation on Rock is scant. It is not mentioned in Domesday but it may be identified with one of the two berewicks (outlying parts of the manor) of Kidderminster called Ribbesford. It appears for the first time in 1210-11 and was afterwards a part of the manor of Ribbesford which was held by the Mortimers of Wigmore.[10]

Of the Romanesque church of St Peter at Rock there remains the south-west corner and north and east walls of the nave plus two bays of the north wall of the chancel.[11] Ashlar construction is used throughout (figs.149) in contrast to both Aston and Kilpeck. The nave is divided into four bays by pilaster buttresses and the chancel is of two bays (fig.149). In the third bay on the north of the nave is a richly carved doorway which is set in a projecting, gabled frame. There is a nook-shafted window in each of the other nave bays and in the chancel east bay, and to the east of the two eastern nave windows there are blind arches. The Romanesque

Fig.149 The Church of St Peter at Rock

corbel table survives but in poor condition. Much of the surface of the north doorway has already flaked away. It has a plain tympanum—which was probably painted—carried on plain jambs with chamfered imposts which continue the foliage trails from the abaci of the other orders (fig.152). The latter are very

Corbels at Rock that invite comparisons with Kilpeck. Fig.150 (top left) appears to be a female exhibitionist figure, like corbel No.28 at Kilpeck (fig.78 top right), whilst Fig.151, a head with a bowl to its mouth (bottom right) is like Kilpeck corbel No.64 (fig.104 bottom left)

Fig.152 Right jamb of the north doorway at Rock Church

close in design to the chancel arch at Shobdon (fig.135) and the south doorway at Rowlstone (fig.178). The next three orders are carried on carved capitals atop plain shafts. The inner capitals take the form of grotesque masks, the next two have paired scallops on each side and what appears to be geometrical interlace on the faces. A frieze of saltire crosses runs across the top of all the capitals. Then come very worn chevron jambs which continue uninterrupted to the impost as at Shobdon (fig.129). In the arch the first order is four-stepped chevron at right angles to the wall with lozenges in the soffit as at Shobdon; order 2 is embattled with flat, affronted, speared chevron in the soffit; order 3 is multiple right-angled chevron with a central channel; order 4 has a row of raised semi-circles as on the chancel arch abaci at Shobdon; order 5 is speared chevron to either side of a thin, angle roll, also paralleled at Shobdon. It is likely that there was also a south doorway to the Romanesque nave, fragments of which have been reset in the north nave wall inside the church. On the nave windows there are traces of ornament on the bases including one with an angle head.

The chancel arch is tall and wide and comprises three orders The bases on the north side are renewed. On the south side the inner base is new but the second base is original and carved with a foliage trail (fig.153). The idea for the richly carved bases is taken from Shobdon where there is also a close parallel for the particular type of foliage trail on the abaci of the third and fourth pillars of the right arch (fig.133, detail reproduced opposite). The outer south base has a series of rolls in an Anglo-Saxon tradition or like the slype arcades at Worcester Cathedral. The various chevrons and the semi-circles on the hood mould belong to the same types as on the north doorway at Rock and the hood

Fig.153 (top) South bases of the chancel arch at Rock. The foliage trail on the inner base compares with that on the abaci of the third and fourth pillars of the right arch at Shobdon (fig.133; detail reproduced on right)

of the chancel arch at Shobdon (fig.135). The outer capitals towards the west are both flanked by square panels carved with geometric interlace (figs.154 & 155). Such panels also appear on the south doorway at Rowlstone (fig.178). The outer left capital has a small, muzzled animal head at the upper angle amidst stylized foliage which spreads over the surface of the capital. The middle capital has three-strand stems which curl into a loose, spiral pattern on both faces. The inner capital has similar, three-strand stems which are loosely interlaced and issue from small angle human heads with characteristic Herefordshire bulbous eyes (damaged at the eastern angle). On the chancel side of the arch there is just one capital which is carved with a demi-figure with a huge head and diminutive body, the arms of which are clad in tight striated folds as on the Shobdon chancel arch knights (figs.137). The figure is flanked by two heads in profile. This capital seems to be by a lesser hand than the others.

The outer right capital of the chancel arch has an angle exhibitionist figure with a malformed body and rubbery limbs (fig.155). The legs are severely bent back and are held with the hands in an acrobatic pose. The foliage interlace cuts through the thigh of the figure, a motif convincingly compared by Zarnecki to the tradition of Germanic animal interlace as, for example, on a drinking horn from the Sutton Hoo ship burial.[12] On the middle capital the body of a centaur is stretched across the bottom half of both faces. The upper body turns to fire an arrow at a stag which runs over the centaur's hind quarters. It will be noticed

Fig.154 (top) North capitals and
Fig.155 (bottom) South capitals to the chancel arch at Rock

that the stag has incredibly long antlers just like those on the penultimate right voussoir on the right arch at Shobdon (fig.130). The west face of the inner capital is carved with three superposed birds of which the largest, at the top, pecks the head of the smallest in the centre of the group. The motif is repeated from corbel No.1 at Kilpeck, the fourth pillar of the chancel arch at Shobdon and the Aston tympanum (figs.61, 141 & 145). At the angle of the capital is a human head with beehive hat, bulbous eyes and a goatee beard. On the main face of the capital is a lion which trots towards the angle head beneath which it droops a paw. It turns to bite its tail which sweeps over its back like the lions on the fourth pillar of the chancel arch at Shobdon (figs.140 & 141). At the eastern angle is a damaged head from which issues three-strand interlace. The eastern capital has a ship with back-turned animal head terminations and a central mast supporting a cross. In the ship are seven human heads and three arms or ropes while above and to either side of the mast are a further two heads and arms. On the east face of the capital is a symmetrical stylized flower with eight lobes.

Throughout this study of the Herefordshire School of sculpture reference has been made to the *Bestiary* as a source for a number of motifs and at Rock two details confirm the connection with this book. The clue comes through the similarity between the ship on the south-east capital of the chancel arch with one on the archivolt of the south doorway at Alne, Yorkshire.[13] At Alne the ship is set beneath an arch on which is inscribed 'A[S]PI[D]O.' The reference, as with the other inscriptions on the Alne doorway, is to the *Bestiary*, in this case to Aspido, the sea monster which 'raises its back above the waves, and it seems to stay in the same place. The winds blow sea-sand on it and it becomes a level place on which vegetation grows. Sailors believe it is an island, and beach their ships on it. Then they light fires, and when the creature feels the heat of the fire, it dives into the water and drags the ship down with it into the depths. The same will befall those who are full of unbelief and know nothing of the wiles of the devil, trusting in him and doing his work; they will be plunged into the fires of Gehenna with him. The nature of the monster is such that when it is hungry it opens its mouth, and gives out a sweet scent; the little fishes smell this and gather in its mouth. When the monster's mouth is full of fishes it closes its jaws and swallows them. The same will befall those who are not firm in their faith, and yield to all delights and temptations as if drunk with scents; and then the devil swallows them up.'[14]

The bowl of the font is contemporary with the Romanesque fabric of the church and is carved with nine medallions filled with stylized foliate forms (fig.156).

Zarnecki attributed the sculpture at Rock to the Aston Master.[15] The parallels noted here between Shobdon, Aston and Rock confirm that attribution and, as at Aston, it seems reasonable to suggest that we are dealing with the patronage of Hugh de Mortimer through the office of Oliver de Merlimond.

Fig.156 The font at Rock Church

RIBBESFORD, Worcestershire, St Leonard

Two manors of Ribbesford are mentioned in Domesday, both berewicks (outlying parts of the manor) of Kidderminster and belonging to the crown. Subsequent to Domesday there is mention of one manor which was held by the Mortimers of Wigmore.[16]

Later the church was enlarged, but the north doorway, the capitals of the south doorway and some fragments of window heads and other details remain from the Romanesque church of St Leonard. The north doorway has two orders with a heavy roll moulding on the inner order and a plain outer order framing a somewhat worn tympanum (fig.157). The heavy roll moulding appears elsewhere in the Herefordshire School on the south doorway at Rowlstone (fig.78) but also occurs outside the school in the south doorway at Bredwardine and the north and south doorways at Martley, Worcestershire. It also appears in other Worcestershire doorways as at Bockleton, Eastham, Knighton-on-Teme and Stoulton,[17] and in the arch to the former eastern chapel of the south transept at Worcester Cathedral (1084-89).[18]

Fig.157 North tympanum at Ribbesford Church

On the left of the Ribbesford tympanum is an archer who leans forward to fire an arrow from a bow set in the middle of the composition at a very plump bird which fills the right side of the tympanum. Beneath the bow there runs a dog(?) which is either on the verge of attacking the archer or running to him for protection from the bird. The archer wears a phrygian cap and has a long, thin head like the Kilpeck knights (fig.36). The long, slim waist and traces of ribbed draperies around the midriff substantiate the comparison. There is a single row of chip-carved saltire crosses around the tympanum like those around the *Agnus Dei* on the Aston tympanum (fig.146).

The capitals and the adjacent carved sections are created from single blocks of stone like the outer west capitals and adjacent interlaced panels on the Rock chancel arch (figs.155 & 158), On the outer left is the motif of the large bird pecking the head of a smaller bird familiar from Kilpeck corbel No.1, the fourth pillar of the chancel arch at Shobdon, the Aston tympanum and the Rock chancel arch (figs.61, 140, 155 & 158). As on the third pillar of the chancel arch at Shobdon (fig.138) fish appear with the birds, just one below the bird at Shobdon, and one above and below at Ribbesford. The inclusion of two fish may signify the waters of Baptism in which case the birds are pelicans and reference to the resurrection is intended. Alternatively, they may be eagles as possibly on the third pillar of the chancel arch at Shobdon, in which case their intention is to inspire the viewer to 'seek out the spiritual fountain of the Lord, and lift up the eyes of your mind to God, who is the fount of justice.'

Fig.158 Left capital to the north doorway at Ribbesford Church

On the capital is a drilled ribbon interlace pattern and a very worn inter-laced design on the truncated panel adjacent to the door. Above the capital and the left block there is a strip of two-strand interlace. The abacus is adorned with four rows of billet ornament in the manner of the three rows on the lintel of the Aston north doorway. On the right capital a variety of inter-lace work enriches the panels and the capitals while the abacus has three rows of chip-carved triangles.

Like the capitals of the north doorway, those of the south doorway were originally flanked by carved panels, but their outer faces are now completely worn away, while the inner faces, like the capitals, are badly eroded. On the left there is geometrically arranged interlace; on the right, a foliage pattern. The right capital is an elaborate version of a volute type with beaded, upright lower leaves and single, broad, striated leaves to either side of the angle volute. Only the inner face is now discernable. The left capital is in worse condition; there appear to be heads meeting at the upper angle and the body and wing of the left bird can still be detected. Below, the forms are too worn to interpret.

Reset inside the blocked south doorway are two shaft fragments with three-strand plait like Kilpeck's west window[19] and, in principle, if not in the exact type of interlace, on the shafts of the left arch at Shobdon (figs.55, 127, 128 & 159). In addition there is a fragment of an abacus with a foliage scroll on the

Fragments of carving reset inside Ribbesford Church.
Fig.159 (top) A shaft fragment with interlace
Fig.160 (left) Three-strand foliage from a hood mould
Fig.161 (right) A fragment of a jamb(?) showing a fleshy foliage trail

upright section and a beaded trail on the chamfer. One fragment is of a hood mould with an undulating, three-strand foliage trail and what appears to be the scales of a dragon's head stop (fig.160). There is also a section of roll moulding like that on the north doorway reset as a segmental blind arch. A fragment of a jamb(?) is set into a niche in the south aisle wall (fig.161). It appears to have a fleshy foliage trail with a single elongated trefoil leaf at the lower right corner, while to the other side are drilled interlaced flat ribbons like the left capital of the north doorway (figs.158 & 161). Further east in the south nave aisle is reset some point-to-point chevron. These fragments suggest that originally there was a rich south doorway and probably an enriched chancel arch in the church. In addition there are three fragments of window heads; two have saltire crosses and incised imitation voussoirs, and one with cable and incised voussoirs. The incised voussoirs are paralleled in the south nave windows at Kilpeck and in the doorway to the former tower stair arch at Dymock, Gloucestershire. The saltire crosses relate to the north tympanum at Aston, but the richness of the window heads is not found elsewhere in the Herefordshire School.

The association of specific motifs at Ribbesford with Aston, Shobdon and Rock suggests that Zarnecki's attribution of Ribbesford to the Aston Master is correct.[20] This may now be tied to the patronage of Hugh de Mortimer with Oliver de Merlimond as executor.

ALVELEY, Shropshire, The Bell Inn

Staffordshire Domesday (8.3) records Alveley as on the land of Earl Roger of Shrewsbury and held by Algar, with eight villagers and a priest. Alveley was a prebend of the college of St Mary Magdalene at Bridgnorth.[21] The college was originally founded at Quatford, just south of Bridgnorth, by Earl Roger of Shrewsbury where a church was dedicated on 22 July 1086. Alveley was given to Quatford and then around 1100 the college moved to Bridgnorth and with it its gifts. There was a close association between the college and the castle at Bridgnorth which seems to have had a part to play in the patronage of the sculpture at Alveley, notably between 1138 and 1140 when Hugh de Mortimer moved into Bridgnorth Castle.[22]

A number of sculptures have been reused in the former Bell Inn at Alveley.[23] Their provenance is not recorded but their connection with the Herefordshire School iconographically and stylistically is unmistakable. Built into the fireplace of the former lounge bar is a knight grappling with interlaced stems like the knights on the second pillar of the chancel arch at Shobdon (figs.137 & 162). Like the knights on the left shaft of the Kilpeck south doorway (fig.36), the one at Alveley wears a phrygian cap and a tight-fitting ribbed tunic. The Alveley knight, unlike his counterparts at Kilpeck, is fully clad in ribbed draperies like the Shobdon knights, but his flared trousers compare with those

Fig.162 (left) Knight at the former Bell Inn, Alveley, grapples with interlaced stems as on a pillar at Shobdon (detail of fig.137, centre), whilst wearing similar cap and trousers to the knights at Kilpeck (detail of fig.36, right)

Fig.163 (left) Carving of a dragon at the former Bell Inn, Alveley, bears comparison with that on the right springer of the south doorway arch at Kilpeck (detail of fig.59)

worn by the knights on Kilpeck corbels No.7 and No.10 (fig.66) and on the latter there are also the horizontal ribs around the midriff as at Alveley. Similar figures also appear at Eardisley, Billesley and Monmouth. The dragon with interlaced body built into an exterior wall parallels the one on the right springer of the second order of the south doorway at Kilpeck (figs.59 & 163). Unlike the latter the upper section of the body of the Alveley dragon is somewhat fatter and has scales in the manner of the dragon on the capital of the first pillar of the chancel arch at Shobdon (figs.136, 142 & 163). Close relatives of the Alveley dragon appear on the font at Chaddesley Corbett, Worcestershire (fig.227).[24]

Two badly weathered panels are each carved with a pair of squat, standing figures under arches; one is now set into a low garden wall, the other in an exterior wall of the inn (fig.164). The closest parallel for the arcaded framing of the figures is in the voussoirs at Brinsop (figs.171, 174 & 175), but in both cases derivation of the squat proportions, the large, egg-shaped heads, hunched shoulders and arms held before the chest is from Shobdon as on the capital of the fifth pillar of the chancel arch (fig.142).

Two further panels are in poor condition and are heavily whitewashed.[25] They appear to be carved with serpents with tightly interlaced bodies in the tradition of the Shobdon serpents and interlaced shafts. Two further panels, also worn and daubed with white-

Fig.164 Badly weathered figures at the former Bell Inn, Alveley

Fig.165 Capital at the former Bell Inn, Alveley

wash, display single-strand interlace as on the third pillar of the left arch and the first and second pillars of the right arch at Shobdon (figs.128 & 137). One panel with concentric interlacing circles may be related to the panels that flank the chancel arch capitals at Rock in design principles (figs.154 & 155). An analogous form flanks the capital which, at the time of my visit in autumn 1997, was kept in the garage (fig.165). The capital is unique in the Herefordshire School in being a carved cushion, a type popular elsewhere in England perhaps not least because of its use in the crypt of Canterbury Cathedral.[26] It is possible that this association is significant for the Alveley capital, but it should not be forgotten that a similar type appeared in the arch to the former south transept chapel at Worcester Cathedral.[27]

The other two Alveley panels are both figurative. One, which is carved with a representation of Samson killing the Lion, is unfortunately covered with thick whitewash (fig.166). The other is a fragmentary winged figure of St Michael killing the dragon of which the upper part of the composition from the chest of St Michael up is lost. The carving of St Michael killing the dragon would have been the largest of the Alveley sculptures; the panel measures 57 x 44.5 cm (fig.242). The scaley body of the dragon relates to Kilpeck corbel No.4 (fig.45), and several examples at Shobdon (figs.154, 160, 166 & 167). St Michael leans forward in the manner of the Alveley fireplace knight and like him is clad in the fashionable ribbed draperies. The double hem lines relate closely to Kilpeck corbel No.10 (fig.66).

The subject matter suggests an ecclesiastical setting while the style and iconography of the Alveley sculptures speak clearly of the Herefordshire School and with the works associated with Hugh de Mortimer and Oliver de Merlimond, but the setting of the work appears to have been different. Other

Carvings of Samson and the Lion
Fig.166 (top left) that at Alveley is closely related to the same subject on the
tympanum at St Mary Magdalene at Stretton Sugwas in Fig.167 (bottom) and,
on a tiny scale, on the abacus of the inner north capital of the west doorway
at Leominster Priory in Fig.168 (top right). In all three, Samson's arms are
held in the same position, he has the same long, slicked-back hair, he wears
the same ribbed garment with tight-fitting tunic and flared trousers. The only
major difference is that the Alveley lion is not elongated like those at Stretton
Sugwas and Leominster, a feature conditioned simply by the shape of the
panel on which it is carved.

than the capital none of the sculpture can be easily connected with a doorway or a chancel arch. It has been suggested that the squat figures under arches should be reconstructed as voussoirs surrounding a tympanum as at Brinsop.[28] However, this is not supported by the shape of the panels, for they do not taper in the manner of voussoirs. In addition, in the panel reset in the garden wall there is the springing of a third arch on the upper left of the panel, whilst a moulded frame at the top of the panel shows no sign of curvature. It follows that placement in a frieze is more plausible for these Alveley pieces. There is both Norman and Anglo-Saxon precedent for this as at Graville-Sainte-Honorine,[29] and Breedon-on-the-Hill, Leicestershire.[30] The best parallel for the variation in the size of the Alveley panels is in the Anglo-Saxon sculpture at St Mary and St Hardulph, Breedon-on-the-Hill.[31] In particular two panels at Breedon-on-the-Hill, each with three standing figures under an arcade, while stylistically far removed from the Alveley pieces, are well-suited to their setting (fig.169). The height of the Alveley panels is 25cm while at Breedon-on-the-Hill it is 20cm.

The Samson and the lion panel measures 55cm wide by 62cm high. The composition does not appear to have been part of a tympanum. Indeed, in spite of the limewash coating there appear to be distinct edges to the frame to the right and left in the manner of frieze sculpture. The St Michael is more difficult to place because only the lower

Fig.169 Anglo-Saxon carved figures at Breedon-on-the Hill Church showing three figures in an arcade, which may be how the Alveley figures were originally set

half of the figure survives, but again there seems to be a vertical frame on the right of the stone. Parallels for St Michael killing the dragon are in a panel reset in the east respond of the north nave arcade at St Leonard at Seaford, Sussex, above the west doorway of St Michael at Garton-on-the-Wolds, Yorkshire, and a relief reset in a niche in the north porch of St Michael at Mere, Wiltshire.

The earliest work in the church of St Mary at Alveley — located about 50 metres to the west of the Bell Inn — is the tower arch which has two orders, the outer one roll moulded, the inner one plain. The second order is carried on a shaft and capital which, on the south, although crude and unfinished depends

Fig.170 South capital of arch between the nave and west tower at Alveley Church

on Herefordshire School traditions (fig.170). Specifically there is a roughed-out angle head from which there grows from the mouth two stems which terminate in trilobed leaves. On the upper part of the capital there is an interlaced frieze. The panel to the left of the capital continues the same stone and has a pointed quatrelobe design inscribed on the surface in preparation for carving in the manner of the capital I saw in the garage and the chancel arch capitals at Rock (figs.154, 155 & 165). The 'frieze' at the top of the capital compares with the north doorway at Ribbesford (fig.158). This suggests that the Bell Inn fragments may have decorated the chancel and or nave of the Norman fabric of the church.

BRINSOP, St George

At Domesday (19.3) Brinsop Manor was held by Alfred of Marlborough, paid tax on five hides of land and included thirty men, eight ploughs and a church. The manor and some of Alfred's other lands, passed to Bernard Neufmarché before 1088. The tithes of the church were given to Brecon Priory around 1100.[32] In 1121 Brinsop Manor and Church went with Bernard's daughter Sybil when she was given by the king in marriage to Miles of Gloucester.[33] Hamer argues that Oliver de Merlimond may have been the tenant at Brinsop for Roger, Earl of Hereford (1143-55), son of Miles of Gloucester. In 1143, the *Wigmore Chronicle* recounts that, after falling out with Hugh de Mortimer, Oliver de Merlimond joined Earl Miles' court at Hereford.[34] Miles was killed in a hunting accident at Christmas 1143, leaving his son, Roger, as earl of Hereford. Oliver remained in Roger's household and may have been the tenant at Brinsop between 1143 and 1159. Amongst the witnesses to Earl Roger's fourth charter to Brecon Priory was one Oliver de Bruneshope,[35] and it is tempting to concur with Hamer's view that this is none other than Oliver de Merlimond.

On the inside of the north nave aisle wall of the parish church of St George at Brinsop, is reset the tympanum of St George killing the dragon which would have been part of the Romanesque church, since replaced by one largely of the

Fig.171 Tympanum of St George killing the dragon at Brinsop Church

fourteenth century (fig. 171). The scaly, serpentine dragon occupies nearly the entire width of the tympanum. It is trampled by St George's horse while its back-turned head, at the lower right of the composition, is speared by the saint's lance. The body of the horse is conveniently elongated to fit the available width of the tympanum; a good example of the abstraction of the figure to conform to the architectural frame, so often evident in Romanesque sculpture.[36] St George wears spurs, flared ribbed trousers, a tight-fitting tunic, a snug cap with flaps that curl up just below the ears, and a voluminous cloak that billows out from his shoulders. A (damaged) bird is perched on St George's left hand in which he holds the reins. A second bird alights on the saint's cloak just behind the shoulder. There are clear traces of red paint on the background which suggest that the tympanum was once fully painted.

The structure of the Brinsop tympanum is related to the tympana at Kilpeck, Pauntley and Dymock (figs.5, 24 & 171). The St George scene and the lower plain area to the left and right are carved from a single stone, while the voussoirs are carved on radiating stones above. St George's flared trousers are the same as those worn by the two knights on Kilpeck corbel No.7 and Samson at Alveley and Stretton Sugwas (figs.166 & 167). The dragon's head, with curled lips, striations and large bulbous eye without a pupil, is virtually identical to those of the serpents on the outer shafts of the Kilpeck south doorway (figs.36 & 171). The dragon's scaly body is the same as Kilpeck corbel No.4 and the Alveley St Michael panel, while the form of the head and the scaly body are found together at Shobdon (figs.128, 136, 142, & 171). The birds are both damaged but enough remains of the one on St George's cloak to relate the crescent wing and straight tail feathers to the birds in medallions on the outer order of Kilpeck south doorway and on the fourth pillar of the chancel arch at Shobdon (figs.32, 140 & 141).

Fig.172 The west front of Parthenay-le-Vieux, a potential source of inspiration for the Brinsop tympanum

The tympanum is traditionally associated with western French sources and in particular with the equestrian figure on the west front of the church at Parthenay-le-Vieux, Vienne (figs.171 & 172).[37] The association seems to be convincing one given the unusual stilted form of the tympana in both places, and the use of radiating figurate voussoirs around the arch at Brinsop, a motif which can only be explained with reference to western French sources either directly or through the Herefordshire intermediary of the Shobdon door-ways (figs.123, 130 & 171).[38] If the latter is the case then the motif was prob-ably transmitted through Oliver de Merlimond.

Convincing as the western French analogue may be for the Brinsop tympanum, it may not tell the whole story. Certain details of the St George composition are allied to cult representations of Mithras slaying the bull. The cave entrance of the cult image has the same stilted appearance as the Brinsop tympanum.[39] The serpentine form, scaly skin and turned-back head of the dragon are all paralleled in the Mithras image at Santa Maria Capua Vetere.[40] The bird perching on the billowing cloak seems to be derived from the Mithras bird behind the cloak, a motif even more closely paralleled in the Mithras cult image at Marino in which there is also a direct analogue for the upturned flaps of Mithras' cap.[41] The inclusion of a pair of fish on one of the Brinsop voussoirs may also reflect a Pisces symbol from a Mithraic model—zodiac signs often appear with the cult image and may even be arranged not unlike radiating voussoirs.[42]

These comparisons between formal elements in the Brinsop tympanum and Italian painted cult images of Mithras raise questions regarding the possible links between the works. It is unlikely that the Brinsop sculptor knew these Italian paintings. Instead, it is possible that there were Roman sources available in England. Mithras slaying the bull from the Walbrook Mithraim bears witness to the existence of sculptured versions of the cult image in England.[43] While the Walbrook image has little in common with the Brinsop St George, it may be significant that the knights on the left jamb of the south doorway at Kilpeck and on a panel at Alveley (figs.36 & 162) wear phrygian caps like the Walbrook Mithras. In the keep of Chepstow Castle there is a reused Roman sculpture which apparently represents a Mithraic scene.[44] In Gloucestershire there are several tombstones with equestrian images in which a prostrate human foe is trampled by the horse and is (or is about to be) speared by the rider. The tombstone of Sextus Valerius Genialis in the Corinium Museum, Cirencester (fig.173), and Rufus Sita in the Gloucester City Museum, are good examples.[45] Also, although geographically removed, there is a Roman relief from Stragglethorpe, Lincolnshire, showing Mars on a horse killing a fish-tailed monster.[46]

The possible source material does not even end here because in representations of hawking for the Labour of the Month of August in medieval

Fig.173 Tombstone of Sextus Valerius, from the Corinium Museum, Cirencester, representing alternative inspiration for the Brinsop tympanum

calendar illustrations a bird rests on the hand of an equestrian figure as in the Brinsop St George.[47] While the representation of the August labour and the Brinsop St George may ultimately derive from the same model and therefore not be directly related, the appearance of the Sagittarius on one of the Brinsop voussoirs suggests knowledge of calendar illustrations. Be that as it may, the sources of the Brinsop tympanum are decidedly eclectic just as they were at Kilpeck and Shobdon. We are not dealing with the product of village stone carvers but the work of sophisticated sculptors who, with their patron, created a current iconography appropriate to the seigneurial knight who at once can be associated with royalty and regional authorities through parallels with the equestrian seals of King Stephen and Miles of Gloucester, Earl of Hereford, 1139-41,[48] and with the crusading warrior saint, a Roman general, and the emperor Constantine, Christ's vicar on earth.

*Fig.174 (top) and
Fig.175 (left)
Detail of voussoirs
on doorway from
north nave aisle to
vestry*

The stilted arch of the tympanum is framed in its upper half with a series of radiating voussoirs carved either singly or in pairs as on the Shobdon doorways (figs.123 & 130). They fit badly and are probably not in their original order.[49] Starting on the left there is a pair of affronted lions followed by some loosely entwined foliage, and then a bird which is closely related to Kilpeck corbel No.1 (fig.61). Next come two rather worn figures standing under arches. They have large, egg-shaped heads and wear ribbed draperies with long, baggy trousers and hold up their arms in front of their chest. They relate to the figures under arches at Alveley. Then come two angels similarly clad in long, baggy trousers who hold books in front of their chests. The final three voussoirs are carved respectively with two fish swimming out as on Kilpeck corbel No.70 (fig.107), foliage interlace, and a lion in profile with head turned *en face*, as on the stem of the Shobdon font.

Fig.176 Panel reset inside the west wall at Brinsop Church

There was evidently more than one doorway to the Romanesque church at Brinsop because above the door that leads from the north nave aisle into the vestry, both inside and out, there are other radiating voussoirs some of which are in a better state of preservation than those above the tympanum. Starting from the left, there is an angel with large wings swooping down from left to right in the manner of the angels on the Ascension/Christ in majesty tympanum at Shobdon (figs.126 & 174). He is clad in a body-hugging garment with alternating wide and narrow ridges. Next are two standing angels with huge, plain wings, egg-shaped heads, bulbous eyes and glum expressions like the chancel arch figures at Kilpeck and those on the capital of the fifth pillar of the chancel arch at Shobdon (figs.119-21, 142 & 174). There follows a mask with two trails of three-strand foliage issuing from the mouth. The next three voussoirs are occupied by a total of six standing figures who are squat relations of the Kilpeck chancel arch figures (fig.175). Each figure is set under a single arch some with big, moulded capitals. The figures hold books in their hands. Like the similar figures above the tympanum they relate closely to Alveley. Above the door from the vestry at left there are two affronted lions which match those to the left of the tympanum. There follows a Sagittarius and a head with foliage issuing from the mouth; a somewhat cut back at the sides and very worn figure of an angel; and two pairs of standing figures of the Kilpeck chancel arch family each of whom holds a book in front of the chest. The last two voussoirs have a foliage-issuing mask and two affronted lions.

There is a fragment of a two-strand, plaited shaft beneath a modern statuette of the Virgin at the north-east angle of the north aisle. This would have come from a doorway, as at Shobdon or a window as in the west window at Kilpeck.

In addition, inside the west wall of the nave is a panel with four beaded medallions set in a square formation each enclosing a bird with a crescent wing and joined by grotesque masks as on the outer order of the south doorway at Kilpeck and the fourth pillar of the chancel arch at Shobdon (figs.40, 107 & 108). Whatever its original function it suggests that the original church was richly decorated.

Many of the parallels cited for the Brinsop sculpture lend credence to its association with the patronage of Oliver de Merlimond. The radiating voussoirs relate to Shobdon and to western France where an analogue is also found for the form and equestrian subject of the tympanum. The squat figures under arches are allied to Alveley where there existed a number of sculptures which did not originate from a doorway, chancel arch or window, as in the Brinsop bird-medallion panel. The complex iconography of the Brinsop tympanum is also appropriate for Oliver de Merlimond who, as Zarnecki suggested, was probably a man of some learning.[50]

To the north-west of the church are the earthworks of a fortified manor house on a moated platform,[51] a juxtaposition of church and fortification as at Kilpeck, and other works of the Herefordshire School including Rowlstone, Castle Frome and Eardisley.

CHAPTER 7

The Lacy Family and Payn Fitz John

Like the churches associated with Hugh de Mortimer and Oliver de Merlimond, those which may be linked with the Lacy family, specifically Sybil de Lacy, and her husband, Payn fitz John, are not precisely documented. Nevertheless, land tenure, circumstantial evidence and the sculpture combine to suggest these candidates as the most likely patrons. It is also argued that Payn fitz John was responsible for building the stone keep at Longtown (Ewyas Lacy) which, in the manner established by Bishop Roger of Salisbury (1102-1139), incorporated sculptural decoration. Whether Payn or Sybil was the patron of the ecclesiastical commissions is uncertain.

ROWLSTONE, St Peter

Domesday (10.1) records the *castellaria* of Ewias Harold where Roger de Lacy held three churches, a priest and thirty-two acres of land. Rowlstone was one of these three churches. In the 1160s the Herefordshire Domesday lists Hugh de Lacy as tenant of Ewyas Harold. It had passed to Payn fitz John between 1115/27 and 1137 through marriage to Sybil de Lacy,[1] and Giraldus Cambrensis[2] described Payn as Lord of Ewyas. Rowlstone was listed as belonging to Llanthony Priory at the Dissolution,[3] although there is no record of the donation in the twelfth century.

The two-bay Romanesque church of St Peter at Rowlstone survives almost complete save the rebuilding of the east wall of the chancel, the addition of the west tower and the south porch, and the insertion of a fifteenth-century window in the south nave wall and one of the nineteenth century in the middle of the north wall of the nave (fig.177). The original work includes the richly carved south doorway and chancel arch (figs.178-81). Both nave and chancel are rubble-built with ashlar quoins and without buttresses, the manner of building at Aston (fig.145) but in contrast to the use of buttresses at Kilpeck (figs.47-8), and the use of ashlar and buttresses at Rock (fig.149). In both the north and south walls

Fig.177 St Peter's Church, Rowlstone

of the chancel there is one small, round-headed Romanesque window, while two similar windows are included in the north wall of the nave. Like the windows at Kilpeck and Aston the heads of those at Rowlstone are created from single stones, although in the chancel a simple roll moulding in inscribed in the head while in the nave the heads are plain.

The south doorway has two orders (fig.178). The heavy roll moulding of the inner order recalls the south doorway at Bredwardine, the north doorway at

Fig.178 South doorway tympanum at Rowlstone Church

Details from figs.140 (left) and 141 (right) showing some of the carvings of birds on the fourth pillar of the chancel arch at Shobdon (after Lewis) and which compare to work at Rowlstone

Martley, Worcestershire, and the north doorway at Ribbesford. It is carried on chamfered abaci carved with a continuous foliage scroll with thin, elongated, trefoil leaves and binding ties which are closely paralleled on the abacus of the fourth pillar of the right arch at Shobdon (figs.140 & 178-9) and the abaci of the chancel arch at Rock (figs.154-5). The capitals are carved on each face with a bird with crescent wing set in foliage interlace. The birds are closely related to those in the medallions of the fourth pillar of the chancel arch at Shobdon (figs.140-1 & 179) and on the outer order of the south doorway at Kilpeck (fig.32). The Rowlstone birds are unusual in having a small disc above the back of each bird which is framed by the back-turned beak and the tail. The outer order has chip-carved, octoprong foliated squares of the same type as those on the right of the lintel of the south doorway at Bredwardine. It is carried on a continuation of the abaci of the inner order beneath which square panels are carved atop square jambs on the same stones as the capitals. The arrangement

recalls the chancel arch at Rock (figs.154-5), the north doorway at Ribbesford (fig.158) and the loose capital at Alveley (fig.165). On the left is a mask encircled by foliage which spews from its mouth, whilst on the right is a square design of four beaded medallions which enclose plain discs and are joined by grotesque masks. Other than the plain discs, the beaded medallions

Fig.179 Right capital to the south doorway at Rowlstone Church, showing the bird design

Fig.180 Left capital of the chancel arch at Rowlstone Church

joined by grotesque masks relate closely to the outer order of the south doorway at Kilpeck, the fourth pillar of the chancel arch at Shobdon, and the Brinsop panel (figs.5, 140-1 & 176).

The Rowlstone tympanum is intimately related to the Christ in Majesty/Ascension at Shobdon (figs.126, 131 & 178). However, it is far better preserved than Shobdon and therefore serves to highlight specific motifs of the Herefordshire School and to suggest something about the training of the Chief Master. The ribbed draperies of Christ, the egg-shaped heads, bulbous eyes and glum expressions of the angels, their tightly clad bodies and layered, flared skirts recall the Kilpeck chancel arch figures (figs.119-21). The emphasised, yet anatomically incorrectly placed ankle bones of Christ recall the misplacement of this feature on the Kilpeck chancel arch figures. The pose of the 'supporting' angels should be compared with an angel on a capital from the east presbytery arch of Hereford Cathedral (fig.11). The egg-shaped head turned full face with bulbous eyes and the basic pose are the same as this Hereford Cathedral angel. The drapery of the Rowlstone angels is more rigid than at Hereford Cathedral and the fluttery quality of the latter reflects an Anglo-Saxon tradition which has been lost at Rowlstone. Taken with the pose of Christ in relation to the God the Father/God the Son capital from the same arch at Hereford Cathedral (fig.134), this serves to suggest that the Chief Master probably had some early experience in the cathedral workshop.

The Rowlstone chancel arch is also original. It has two orders carried on capitals like those of the south doorway, with one bird in foliage on each side facing the angle. Carved on the same stone as each capital there is a panel with two figures facing the nave (figs.180-1). On the north there is an angel carrying a cross in his right hand and a book in his left, and a haloed figure with a staff terminating in a cross head in his right hand and a book held in front of his shoulder in the left. On the south the figures are carved upside down; to the outside an angel with a scroll held before the legs with the right hand and a book raised before the chest in the left, while to the inside a haloed figure grasps a short-stemmed cross in the right hand and a book in the left. The inversion of the figures is an appropriate reference to St Peter who was cruci-fied upside down (fig.181).[4] The figures are most closely allied to Shobdon in particular the capital of the fifth pillar of the chancel arch, the angel immediately to the right of centre on the second order of the right

Fig.181 Right capital of the chancel arch at Rowlstone Church

arch (figs.130 & 142). In general type they may also be compared with a number of the Brinsop voussoir figures but in this instance one is aware of the more robust character of the Brinsop sculptures especially evident in a compar-ison of the heads (figs.174-5). While the Brinsop sculptures came from the hand of the Chief Master, the Rowlstone chancel arch capitals have the reserve of the Aston Master or perhaps an assistant. The abaci of the capitals are carved with a repetitive bird motif, appropriate to St Peter with reference to the cock crowing. On the chamfer of the abaci are heart-shaped, striated leaves which frame discs, a motif which also makes a fleeting appearance on the otherwise unornamented chancel arch of St Mary at Cusop.[5] The sculpture of the abaci continues to the side walls of the nave as a decorated string course with animals which is unusual, but is paralleled on the apse external string course at Aulnay-de-Saintonge.[6]

The wooden barrel vault in the chancel may reflect the twelfth-century stone barrel vault in the Lacy church of Kempley, Gloucestershire, and the nave of Romanesque Tewkesbury.[7]

To the north-east of the church the former castle is represented by the tump, another case of the pairing of church and castle.

LONGTOWN CASTLE

The round keep of Longtown Castle (Ewyas Lacy), is normally dated to the late twelfth century on the basis of a reference in the Pipe Roll for 1187. Round keeps are also generally associated with the late twelfth and thirteenth centuries.[8] However, the round keep at New Buckenham, Norfolk, must have

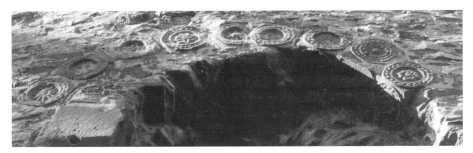

Fig.182 Detail of east window at Longtown Castle with the, almost certainly, reset medallions

been completed by 1146 when William of Albini II gave his former castle at Old Buckenham to the Augustinians so that they might use its masonry to build their abbey.[9] Is it possible to date the Longtown keep that early and perhaps even associate it with the Lord of Ewyas, Payn fitz John? The question deserves further research. In the present work the investigation is confined to the beaded medallions in the arch of the east window which relate closely to fragments from Hereford Cathedral[10] and the east arch and south clerestory window of the presbytery at Llandaff Cathedral commenced in 1120 (fig.41). Payn is listed as a magnate of the diocese of Llandaff in 1119,[11] making it feasible for Payn to have seen the design there. Two of the medallions at Longtown are damaged and are placed too close to each other which suggests that the windows have in fact been widened and the medallions inserted, being taken from an earlier building. In most cases where carvings are reused, the carvings have not travelled far, suggesting that they were originally set in some part of the structure of the castle, or perhaps a local chapel.

HEREFORD, St Giles Hospital Church

Hamer unearthed evidence to connect St Giles Hospital Church with the Lacy family. Between 1141 and 1155 Earl Roger of Hereford granted to St Guthlac's Priory in Hereford all the land of the fee of Walter de Lacy outside St Owen's Gate.[12] Thus the land was in the Lacy family and would have been under the charge of Payn fitz John 1115/21-37 and Sybil de Lacy, patrons of Rowlstone Church.

A weather-worn tympanum depicting Christ in Majesty/Ascension is built into the west wall of St Giles' Hospital on St Owen Street outside St Owen's Gate (fig.183). Presumably it came from the chapel of St Giles' Hospital, the round nave of which (suggesting a Knights Templar origin) was uncovered in 1927 when the church built on the site in 1682 was demolished.[13] It is of the same type as Shobdon and Rowlstone (fig.178), except that it is surrounded by a single order arch with interlace carved on the same stone as the tympanum.

Close by, built into the wall of the Williams Almshouses facing the street, there is a worn and heavily whitewashed double capital carved with a central figure between two animals

Fig.183 Weather-worn tympanum from St Giles

which has been identified as Christ as the Good Shepherd.[14] A plaster cast of this capital, taken when it was in better condition, is preserved in St Leonard's,

Fig.184 Plaster cast of St Giles' capital preserved at Ribbesford Church

Ribbesford. Worcestershire (fig.184). The large, egg-shaped head and staring eyes recall the Brinsop voussoir figures (fig.175), though the thin waist and billowing skirt of the St Giles Christ are not like the Brinsop figures. Comparison with Lewis' lithograph suggests a general similarity to some of the figures on the second order of the right arch at Shobdon (fig.130). Turning to the cast of this Shobdon arch, there is a remarkably close parallel for the thin waist and billowing skirt in voussoir No.13 (No.14 in the cast) at the apex of the arch. Parallels for the sheep are not encountered within the Herefordshire School but it should be noted that both sheep raise their front leg nearest the background, like the lions and stags on the second order of the Shobdon right arch (fig.130). The capital is therefore the work of the Herefordshire School.

Also built into the same wall of the Williams' Almshouses is a grotesque corbel which is just as weathered as the double capital and, like it, is heavily whitewashed (fig.185). Enough detail remains, however, in the detailing of the eyes to suggest comparison with the heads on the vault boss of the apse at Kilpeck (fig.13).

CASTLE FROME, St Michael

Domesday (10.30) records that Castle Frome was held by Roger de Lacy. It was given by Hugh de Lacy to St Peter's, Gloucester,[15] and was inherited by Payn fitz John 1115/21-1137 through marriage to Sybil de Lacy. It then passed to Roger, son of Miles of Gloucester, and his wife, Cecily, daughter of Payn fitz John and Sybil de Lacy.[16]

Fig.185 Heavily whitewashed corbel from St Giles', Hereford

The church of St Michael at Castle Frome was probably conceived at the same time as the castle located 350 yards to the east.[17] According to Pevsner,[18] the church is 'early Norman,' but the font is later, 'one of the masterworks of Romanesque sculpture in England.' Architecturally the Romanesque fabric of the church is plain—comprising a two-cell plan with a square-ended chancel, and a rectangular nave (fig.186). The original fabric is of rubble and small squared stones but ashlar is used for a pilaster in the middle of the west gable and for the window frames, one in the west wall, one in the south wall of the nave and two in the north. The technique is the same as in the apse at Kilpeck even to the use of a single stone for the window heads, and the continuation of the buttress stones into the plane of the wall. There are west and south doorways with large, plain lintels cut from single stones, and tympana of three courses of ashlar. The priest's doorway in the south wall of the chancel has a plain head with a single stone in which a plain tympanum is recessed. It is likely that the plain tympana would have been painted like that inside the west end of the nave at St-Savin-sur-Gartempe, Vienne (*see rear cover*), and it is significant that a plain tympanum is

Fig.186 St Michael's Church, Castle Frome

used above the west doorway of St Mary's, Kempley, Gloucestershire, a Lacy church which is famous for its painted chancel. The chancel arch at Castle Frome has a single order and rests on chamfered imposts in which there are several horizontal incisions.

All this contrasts with the font which, with that at Eardisley, are the richest of the Herefordshire School (fig.187 *and front cover*). The huge bowl is 'supported' on three crouching figures clad in ribbed draperies, like the knights on the Kilpeck south doorway and the Shobdon chancel arch (figs.36 & 137). Just one head remains whose bulging eyes and curly hair and beard are closely related to corbels No.88 and No.89 on the west wall at Kilpeck (figs.120 & 121). The rim of the font is carved with symmetrical, three-strand interlace, while the stem is covered with irregular, loose, single-strand interlace, a vine which protects the figures above.

The main scene on the bowl is the Baptism of Christ in which there is an oversize figure of St John the Baptist to the left of the relatively tiny Christ who is caught in the swirling tide of the Jordan with four large fish. The hand of God, above, and, the dove of the Holy Spirit, to the right, complete the Trinity (Fig.188). Affiliations for the draperies of John the Baptist and details of the head types are found with the Kilpeck chancel arch figures (figs.119-21). The nail-head-like appearance of John the Baptist's ankle bone and his huge, rubbery feet with elongated toes are related to the Rowlstone Christ (fig.178). The pose and proportions of John the Baptist derive from the bearded angel on one of the capitals of the east presbytery arch at Hereford Cathedral (fig.189),[19] supporting the suggestion that the early experience of the Chief Master was in the Hereford Cathedral workshop in the time of Bishop Reynhelm, 1107-15.[20]

To the right of the Baptism are two pecking birds which are closely related to the pair at the bottom of the right shaft of the Kilpeck south doorway and have been identified as doves which may symbolize purity after Baptism (fig.190).[21]

Fig.187 The font at Castle Frome Church

The font at Castle Frome Church
This page: Fig.188 (top) Detail of the baptism of Christ; Fig.189 (above left)
Detail of bearded angel on a capital from the east presbytery arch of
Hereford Cathedral; Fig.190 (above right) Detail of birds.
Opposite page: Fig.191 (top) Detail of the bull of St Luke; Fig.192 (centre)
Detail of the lion of St Mark and eagle of St John; Fig.193 (bottom) Detail of
of the angel of St Matthew

121

Alternatively, they they may be explained with reference to the pelican as described in the *Bestiary* in association with the Resurrection. Their inclusion on the Castle Frome font would therefore refer to the belief of rebirth through Baptism.[22]

Next to the birds, facing east, is the bull of St Luke (fig.191), followed by the lion of St Mark (fig.192), the eagle of St John and the angel of St Matthew (fig.193). Of these the lion must be by the same hand as those on the stem of the Shobdon font. The pose of the angel and the tiered skirt relate closely to the Rowlstone tympanum (fig.178) on which we also encounter the emphasised ankle bones.

Fig.194 The font at Freudenstadt, Würtemberg

The 'support' figures of the font may be generally associated with Italy. However, a link with Germany should not be overlooked. Robert de Losinga's Bishop's Chapel at Hereford Cathedral established links with Germany in the late eleventh century which may have accounted for the former eastern towers in the Romanesque cathedral.[23] In the light of this it is interesting that the 'support' figures, arranged like those on the Castle Frome font, occur on the fonts at Freckenhorst, Westphalia, and Freudenstadt, Würtemberg (fig.194).[24] Furthermore, in Hereford Cathedral itself there are four demi-figures of lions at the base of the font, albeit heavily restored, and similar lions appear at the base of the font at Sutton St Michael.[25]

CHAPTER 8

The Patronage of Ralph de Baskerville

A papal Bull of Pope Innocent II, dated 30 April 1142, records the gift of the churches of Eardisley, Stretton Sugwas, and other churches and chapels on the land of Ralph de Baskerville, to Llanthony Secunda, an Augustinian house located just outside Gloucester.[1] This was founded by Miles of Gloucester in 1137 to remove many of the canons of Llanthony Prima from their politically troubled situation in Monmouthshire.[2] Domesday (10.46) records that Robert de Baskerville held Eardisley and two and a half hides at Stretton Sugwas (10.24) and other land from Roger de Lacy. Like Payn fitz John and Miles of Gloucester, the character of the Baskervilles in the twelfth century is not reported favourably. It is reputed that Henry II said that 'if there were only one Baskerville left in Christendom, that would suffice to corrupt the whole mass of humanity,' while the 'degeneracy' of Gerald de Barry, nephew of Giraldus Cambrensis, was ascribed by that chronicler to his descent on his mother's side from the Baskervilles.[3]

EARDISLEY, St Mary Magdalene

The chalice-shaped font at Eardisley is carved with a tightly woven, two-strand interlace on the rim, a cable neck and angular, two-strand interlace on the splayed foot (fig.195). The angular type of interlace compares with that on a pre-Conquest stone at Llantwit Major and indicates, as at Shobdon, that the new Norman rulers assimilated regional artistic traditions into their repertoire.[4] On the bowl of the font there are two knights dressed in tight-fitting, ribbed tunics, the flared trousers of which descend to just below the knee (fig.195). They have thin, pointed faces with large, bulbous eyes and wear pointed

Fig.195 (top) the font at Eardisley Church, showing the two knights fighting and entwined in stems
Fig.196 (bottom left) and Fig.197 (bottom right) show the Harrowing of Hell, with a figure to the left of Christ

helmets. The knight on the right spears his opponent through the thigh, whilst the left hand knight wields a sword over his right shoulder. The knights are entwined in thin stems. Like the Kilpeck knights on the left main shaft of the south doorway (fig.36) and the knight at Alveley (fig.162), they struggle against the evil forces of the entwining stems. They compare favourably with the figures on Kilpeck corbel No.10 (fig.66), and at Shobdon on the second pillar of the left arch (fig.127) and the second pillar of the chancel arch (fig.137). It has been suggested that the scene may represent the duel in 1127 between Sir Ralph de Baskerville and his father-in-law, Lord of Clifford Castle.[5] The dispute arose when Clifford 'rudely and unjustly' dispossessed Baskerville of some property,[6] resulting in a duel fought outside Hereford in which Clifford was killed. Baskerville subsequently purchased the Pope's pardon for killing his own father-in-law.

To the right of the knights is an idiosyncratic representation of the Harrowing of Hell (figs.196 & 197). The theme is adapted from the tympanum of the north doorway at Shobdon (fig.125). The composition is centred around the cross which Christ, who moves in from the right even more swiftly than at Shobdon, plants with His right hand. Unlike Shobdon, Christ does not thrust the cross into the mouth of hell but rather the cross is flanked by interlace. As at Shobdon, Christ drags a figure up with a swift diagonal motion. The Shobdon figure has been identified as Adam following the standard iconography of the scene, but the Eardisley figure, who is half the size of Christ, is clothed while Adam is usually depicted as naked. The interlace that surrounds this figure is to be equated with hell. A dove perches on Christ's upper arm. To the left of Christ is a standing figure in dynamic pose with rubbery arms and his right hand placed on his waist while with his left he holds a closed book in front of his chest. All three figures are clothed in ribbed draperies like the Shobdon knights (figs.127 & 137) although only 'Adam' wears the knightly trousers while the other two have robes. This contemporary reference to the knight may be intended as Ralph de Baskerville. The third figure in the scene has been identified as God the Father,[7] Thus we have a blend of the Trinity which is completed at Eardisley with the dove on Christ's arm. The Trinity has a long association with representations of the Baptism in which the hand of God and the dove of the Holy Ghost appear above the head of Christ, as on the Castle Frome font (fig.188).

The theme of the Harrowing of Hell is unique to Eardisley on English fonts but is not difficult to interpret. After the Crucifixion Christ descended into hell but rose again on the third day. Just as Adam is saved from hell and thereby like Christ is reborn in heaven, so through Baptism one simulates the death and

Resurrection of Christ and, like Adam, has the sins cleansed and is reborn.[8] The chalice shape of the font also fits in with this to combine the sacraments of Eucharist and Baptism.[9]

Fig.198 The lion on the Eardisley font

Behind the interlace of hell at the back of the Harrowing scene there is a lion in profile with head turned *en face* (fig.198). This is similar to the lions on the stem of the Shobdon font as is the raised leg with the drooping paw nearest the background, as indeed elsewhere in the Herefordshire School. Iconographically the Eardisley lion should be interpreted as evil because it is entangled in stems and Ralph de Baskerville is being saved from the lion, just as he is being saved from Hell.

Although Eardisley church does not preserve any Romanesque fabric *in situ*, there is, in addition to the font, one Romanesque fragment which indicates that originally it was a richly decorated member of the Herefordshire School, like Shobdon and Kilpeck (fig.199). The fragment in question is part of a shaft which is carved with the top of a human head flanked by foliage. The shape of the head and the huge bulbous eyes without pupils immediately relate the work

Fig.199 Part of a human head together with foliage, being a fragment of a romanesque shaft from Eardisley Church

to the font (albeit a different hand) and further to the figurated shafts of the Shobdon left arch (south doorway) and chancel arch (figs.127 & 137). Thus, as at Shobdon and on the south doorway at Kilpeck, there would have been figures of knights as appropriate for the church of the local lord.

In addition to the parallels cited above, the heads of the Eardisley knights and the ribbed, flared trousers should be compared with the capital in the western bay of the north nave triforium at Tewkesbury (fig.17).[10] It

126

has already been suggested that the Chief Master may have worked at Tewkesbury Abbey before being employed at Kilpeck. This parallel with the Eardisley knights serves to confirm the Chief Master's activity at that great Benedictine abbey.

The castle at Eardisley, 50 yards west of the church,[11] includes a motte and bailey earthworks. Once again there is a classic siting of church and castle close in form to Kilpeck, even though the castle may not have been stone-built.[12]

It seems plausible to suggest that not only would the church have been completed by 1142 but that it was done before the outbreak of the Welsh rebellion and civil war after the death of Henry I in 1135.

STRETTON SUGWAS, St Mary Magdalene

Fig.167 (top) the Samson and Lion tympanum at Stretton Sugwas, which has been compared with that in the right arch of the west front at Parthenay-le-Vieux, Deux Sevres, western France, Fig.200 (below)

The Samson and the Lion tympanum is the only feature of the Romanesque church of St Mary Magdalene at Stretton Sugwas to have survived (fig.167). It is reset above a doorway in the north wall of the nave of the 1880 church opposite the south doorway. Like the Brinsop tympanum it has been allied with western France and in particular with the tympanum in the right arch of the west front at Parthenay-le-Vieux, Deux-Sevres (fig.200).[13] The parallel is entirely convincing and may be explained through Oliver de Merlimond's pilgrimage to Santiago-de-Compostella on which he passed through western France.[14] In composition it is in many respects a mirror image of Brinsop. The lion trots with Brinsop-like dressage precision and is elongated to fit the width available, the paw nearest the background is raised to fill what would otherwise be a void, while the lion's tail at Stretton Sugwas flips up to fill the space occupied by St George's cloak at Brinsop. Otherwise the composition relates intimately to the Samson and the Lion at Alveley. In terms of style the flared, ribbed trousers of Samson relate to the Brinsop St George, Kilpeck corbel No.7, and the knights on the Eardisley font (fig.195). The Eardisley knights also sport the same tight-fitting tunic as Samson and have similar elongated heads, beards and moustaches. The lion's head and the drooping paw closest to the background go with the left capital of the Kilpeck south doorway (fig.41). All this serves to attribute the Stretton Sugwas tympanum to the Chief Master working, as at Eardisley, for Ralph de Baskerville.

Fig.201 Tympanum and lintel on the north doorway at Bredwardine Church

The crudely executed, hollow-chamfered hood mould of the tympanum is terminated on two human heads. At the bottom of the tympanum there is a rope moulding. The heads were not carved by the Chief Master which raises an interesting question concerning the division of labour within the workshop. The rope moulding gives an important clue because it also appears on the otherwise unadorned tympana of the north and south door-ways at Mathon[15] and on the lower angle of the lintel of the north doorway at Bredwardine (fig.201). This suggests that there were clear divisions of labour in the Herefordshire School and that the Chief Master was only involved with what was deemed to be the most important sculpture.

CHAPTER 9

The Patronage of William Fitz Baderon of Monmouth

In Herefordshire Domesday (1.48) Monmouth Castle is recorded as belonging to the king, under the charge of William son of Baderon. The priory church of St Mary at Monmouth was founded by William fitz Baderon before 1086 as a dependency of St Florent, Saumur[1] and was dedicated in 1101-2.[2] Robert de Bethune, Bishop of Hereford, confirmed the earlier donations at the request of Baderon of Monmouth.[3] The secular and monastic foundations conform to the pattern established in the region at Chepstow by William fitz Osbern immediately after the Conquest. Subsequently, Monmouth Castle chapel was also given by William fitz Baderon II to St Florent at Saumur.[4]

MONMOUTH

The Romanesque tympanum now preserved in the Monmouth Museum is without provenance other than that it was built into the Williams Brothers shop in Monmouth (fig.202).[5] It depicts a pair of figures like the fighting knights on the Eardisley font (fig.195). Unlike Eardisley, however, the Monmouth knights carry no weapons but have rubbery arms one of which 'punches' the opponent, while the other is intertwined in foliage and grabs at a stem. In this respect the closest parallel is with the knights on Kilpeck corbel No.10 (fig.66). Once again we meet the familiar theme of knights grappling with the forces of evil as elsewhere in the Herefordshire School— as on the left jamb of the south doorway at Kilpeck (fig.36) and at Alveley (fig.162). Although the arc of the tympanum is unusual, the truncation of the top is like the Kilpeck tympanum—a technical detail to further ally the

129

*Fig.202 Tympanum of two knights from
the castle chapel(?), now held in
Monmouth Museum, compared with the knights
on Eardisley font (below, detail from fig.195)*

Monmouth work to the Herefordshire School.

It is unlikely that such a subject would have come from the local priory church but it may have been in the castle chapel. It was suggested above that Payn fitz John may have been responsible for the decoration at Longtown Castle, and it is possible that at Monmouth Castle William fitz Baderon introduced some enrichment. The keep is partially preserved and is of rubble construction with ashlar quoins and window frames. Two heads are preserved at the top of the east wall (fig.203) and, although they are very worn, they show that decoration embellished the keep.

A capital recently found in the west tower of the Benedictine alien priory of the Blessed Virgin Mary and St Florent, Monmouth, suggests that Herefordshire School sculptors worked there (fig.204). Presumably from the west portal, the capital is carved with foliage on beaded stems of the same type as the Kilpeck tympanum (fig.5) and one of the Hereford

Cathedral crossing capitals (fig.6). There is also a triple-scalloped capital (fig.205) reused as the base of a stoup that is allied to the apse capitals at Kilpeck (fig.4) and the nave triforium capitals at Gloucester Cathedral. The flanks of the original west front still survive and, on the south side, there is a chevron string course (fig.206) of the same type as on the cornice

Fig.203 The worn heads on the east wall of Monmouth Castle

of the Fownhope tower (fig.225). To the north there is a string course with the stepped motif (fig.207) close to that used beneath volutes on the capitals of the south doorway at Pauntley (fig.24), and in the scallop faces of a nave arcade capital at Hereford Cathedral.[6] The west respond of the nave arcade also survives with a large cylindrical pier—a scaled-down version of those in the Hereford Cathedral nave.

Fig.204 (left) Detail of capital from Monmouth Priory
Fig.205 (above) Scalloped capital from Monmouth Priory reused as the base of a stoup

RUARDEAN, St John the Baptist

Domesday Herefordshire (15.2) lists Ruardean on the land of William son of Baderon and held by Solomon. Wihenoc received Monmouth from William I

Fig.206 (top) Detail of chevron string course and
Fig.207 Detail of string course, both on the west front of Monmouth Priory

and upon Wihenoc's retirement to the abbey of St Florent at Saumur, as a monk, the property was inherited by his nephew, William fitz Baderon II. Although there is no specific mention of Ruardean church it is likely that it was included with William fitz Baderon's gift to St Florent of Saumur of 'the church of Monmouth and all their churches.'[7]

The tympanum over the south doorway depicts St George killing the dragon, the knight triumphing over evil, and is closely allied to the Brinsop tympanum (figs.171 & 208). As at Brinsop, St George rides from left to right on a horse whose body is conveniently elongated to fit the available space of the tympanum. He wears flared, ribbed trousers to just below the knee, has spurs, and a cloak billows out behind him. He holds the reins high on the horse's neck with his left hand and with the right he thrusts the spear into the mouth of the dragon which looks more like a serpent with a scaly body that extends under, and is trampled by, the horse. There are no radiating voussoirs like Brinsop and generally the tympanum is less accomplished and is probably the work of an assistant of the Chief Master.

Fig.208 Tympanum of St George and the Dragon on the south doorway of Ruardean Church, Gloucestershire

GOODRICH CASTLE

Strictly speaking the keep of Goodrich Castle lies outside the parameters of the Herefordshire School of Sculpture. However, there is good reason to associate Goodrich keep with a patron of the Herefordshire School. In the absence of substantive remains of the castles of Kilpeck, Shobdon, Castle Frome, Eardisley and Rowlstone, it serves to illustrate the duality of the secular and the sacred in the patronage of the new Norman lords which is already experienced at Monmouth under William fitz Baderon.

Godric's Castle is mentioned in 1101-2 but this is generally considered too early for the present keep.[8] On the other hand, *c*.1160-70 or even a mid-twelfth-century date seems too late.[9] It has been equated with William (II) fitz Baderon, Lord of Monmouth, who seized the castle during the anarchy of King Stephen 1135-54 (Pettifer 1995, 96). Numerous features relate the stonework of the keep to the churches associated with the Dymock School and St Peter's, Gloucester, even if the flourishes of adorning sculpture are absent:

1. The pilaster buttresses have stones that continue into the main plane of the wall as in the nave of Dymock and in the buttresses at Kilpeck.

2. The hollow roll moulding on the window jambs is the same as on the jambs of the south doorway at Dymock.

3. The chevron jambs of the window (fig.209) are paralleled on the south doorway of St Michael at Bulley, Gloucestershire.

4. The chevroned string course at the sill level of the upper windows is a simpler version of the one on the upper south section of the west front of Monmouth Priory).

5. The multi-scalloped right capitals of the doorway have V-necking as on the upturned capital of the pillar piscina at Monmouth Priory).

6. The tympanum above the doorway that leads from the first floor chamber to the staircase is constructed with the same stone as the lintel and the latter spreads further to the left and right exactly as in the tympana of the south doorways at Dymock, Pauntley and Kilpeck.

Fig.209 Chevron jambs on the north window on the keep at Goodrich Castle

This suggests that the Goodrich keep was executed by masons who were also involved with church building in the region and should be be dated *c.*1120-40. In 1144 William fitz Baderon II, Lord of Monmouth, records that he granted the church of St Giles of Goodrich Castle to the Priory of St Mary of Monmouth.[10] Nothing remains of the Romanesque fabric of Goodrich Church but William's gift suggests that he was involved in its (re)construction. The motifs on the castle relate to Monmouth, the Herefordshire School and associated works and imply William's involvement there. The castle and church were probably built together early in King Stephen's reign.

CHAPTER 10

Leominster Priory

Leominster is recorded in Domesday (1.10a) as held by the king and having six priests. The priory was refounded in 1123 by Henry I from Reading Abbey and the nave of this Romanesque church survives along with with the west front. The eastern arm, crossing and transepts of the church are known from excavation.[1] There was an apse-ambulatory plan with three radiating chapels, aisleless transepts with one chapel each to the east. There is sculpture on the capitals of the west doorway and the west window both inside and out, plus a single head at the north-west angle of the north wall of the nave aisle.

The west doorway is pointed and has five orders. The ninety-degree multiple chevron on the fourth order and the flat chevron of the hood mould account for the only carving in the arch (fig.210). Plain orders mixed with carved orders appear in western France and find regional parallel in the chapter house doorway at Gloucester Cathedral. It is possible that the plain orders were painted like the triforium bays towards the west end of the south side of the nave, and later on the south doorway of the Lady Chapel at Glastonbury Abbey.[2] Orders 1, 2 and 6 are carried on plain jambs but orders 3-5 have capitals and richly carved abaci atop coursed shafts on beak-spur bases. The capitals are all symmetrically carved. On the inner left are two serpents entwined in thick branches of foliage (fig.211). They are slimmer relations of the serpent on the capital of the third pillar of the left arch at Shobdon (fig.128). The middle left capital has two men dressed in one-piece ribbed suits and 'beehive' hats who cut through entwining foliage. The men's bodies are in profile, but their large-egg-shaped heads are full-face in the manner of St John the Baptist on the Castle Frome font (fig.188). They belong to the same family as the figures entwined in stringy stems on the second pillar of the chancel arch and the second pillar of the left arch at Shobdon (figs.127 & 137). On the outer left capital two birds face the angle. They are also entwined in foliage but their heads emerge free at the top corner of the capital. They are closely related to the birds with straight wings and raised leg nearest the back-ground on the Castle Frome font (fig.190).

On the right splay of the doorway, the inner capital is carved with three rows of stylized foliage which have no parallel elsewhere in the Herefordshire School (fig.211). Two affronted lions with big, floating

Fig.210 The west doorway of Leominster Priory Church

paws and large heads turned *en face* are on the middle capital. They are closely related to those on the Shobdon and Eardisley fonts (figs.198), The outer capital has two horizontal rows of undulating stringy foliage and elongated trefoil leaves as on the abaci of the capitals of the third and fourth pillars of the right arch at Shobdon and the abaci of the chancel arch capitals at Rock (figs.133 & 165).

Fig.211 The left capitals of the west doorway to Leominster Priory Church

Fig.212 The left capital of the west window of Leominster Priory Church

The left capitals should probably be interpreted in a similar way to that suggested by George Zarnecki for the Billesley, Warwickshire, tympanum.[2] The men, pursued by evil serpents, struggle to escape towards the doves, symbols of purity, by cutting themselves from the ensnaring branches. The right side is less straightforward although the lions are probably evil, like the one on the left capital of the south doorway at Kilpeck (fig.56). The abaci are all richly carved with a row of beads on the upper face, and triangular, three-leaf palmettes divided by beads on the chamfered face. The outer right abacus has a chevron-like, double rope moulding on the face and overlapping, half rosettes on the chamfer.

The left capital of the west window has eight birds in beaded medallions joined by grotesque masks as on the Brinsop panel, Kilpeck south doorway and the fourth pillar of the Shobdon chancel arch (figs.32, 140, 176 & 212). Both faces of the right capital are carved with a large bird perched on the back of a smaller bird whose head it pecks in the manner of Kilpeck corbel No.1, the fourth pillar of the chancel arch at Shobdon, and elsewhere (figs.61, 140 & 213). Stylized symmetrical flower motifs adorn the abaci while the adjacent string courses have a simple, incised chevron.

Facing north at the north-west angle of the north aisle wall is a humanoid head with large eyes with drilled pupils, a flared, foliage-like moustache, and a gaping mouth from which spew stunted stems or serpents (fig.214) Both the

Fig.213 The right capital of the west window of Leominster Priory Church

foliate and demonic find parallels in the heads of the second order of the Kilpeck south doorway (figs.20-1). For the setting of the head, the closest parallels known to me are on the angles of the nave at Kilmalkedar, County Kerry. A number of motifs used at Kilmalkedar, as at Cormac's Chapel, County Tipperary, reflect west of England and Welsh sources, not least in Herefordshire and Gloucestershire, and in this connection reference may be made to the twin-headed corbels at the eastern angles of the chancel at Cradley, Herefordshire, and the north-west corner of the nave at Preston near Dymock, Gloucestershire.[4] Furthermore, at the western angles of the nave of St James, Tedstone

Fig.214 Head at north-west corner of north nave

Delamere, Herefordshire, there are uncarved projections which seem to be typological forerunners of this motif. It is possible that at Leominster we have a stone version of a head carved on the end of a beam in a wooden, or half-timbered building.

The west doorway of Leominster Priory is unusual in having carved capitals on the interior as well as the exterior. On the south side the outer capital has loose, single-strand interlace similar to that used on the first and second pillars of the right arch at Shobdon (figs.131 & 215). On the inner capital vines issue from a human mask with biforkated, plaited beard (fig.215). On the north side the outer capital has inter-penetrating, two-strand circles, while on the inner capital a grotesque angle mask

Fig.215 (top) Inner south capitals and Fig.216 (lower) Inner north capitals of the west doorway at Leominster Priory Church

spews rather disorderly, leafless vines (fig.216). As on the exterior the abaci are carved; on the left with palmettes and symmetrical flowers, while on the north the inner abacus is plain and the outer one starts with saltire cross and palmette which soon gives way to a fleshy interlace above striated heart scrolls like those on capitals at Dymock and Kempley,[5] with a Samson and the Lion of the left, a miniature version of the same theme at Alveley and Stretton Sugwas (figs.166, 167 & 168).

The single order of the interior of the west window is also carried on carved capitals. On the south there is a multi-scallop capital with an incised trail on the faces and stylized foliage abacus (fig.217). The north capital is a double scallop with V-necking with, on the south face, a beaded outline to the left and a four-sided, hollowed lobe within a circle to the right, and on the east face, a six-pronged star to the left and a simple pattern to the right (fig.218). The abacus is richly decorated with a number of motifs and a simply executed human head at the angle. Of these motifs the four-sided, hollowed lobe within a circle is of unusual interest. It is not a common motif. On the one hand, it is found on a fragment preserved in the presbytery gallery of Gloucester Cathedral (fig.219), and on the lintel of the south doorway at Pauntley (fig.24), and therefore it may simply substantiate connections between Gloucester, the Dymock School and the Herefordshire School. On the other hand, it is used at Old Sarum,[6] at Reading Abbey, on the label of the arcade in the ringing chamber of the crossing tower of Winchester Cathedral, on the label of the main arcade in the presbytery of

The west window at Leominster Priory Church. Fig.217 (top) The inner south capital; Fig.218 (centre) The inner north capital; Fig.219 (bottom) A similar motif to that on the north capital found at Gloucester Cathedral

Romsey Abbey (fig.220) and the label of the west doorway of Porchester Priory (fig.221). Reading Abbey was founded by Henry I and royal patronage is probable for the rebuilding after the collapse of the crossing tower at Winchester in 1107. Matilda stayed at Romsey before her marriage to Henry I in 1100 and it seems likely that the present church was commenced around 1120 with royal financing.[7] Porchester Priory was founded by Henry I in 1133 and Old Sarum was rebuilt by Bishop Roger (1102-39) who was also the royal justiciar and therefore a close associate of the

Fig.220 (top) The motif is also found at Romsey Abbey, in the north arcade of the presbytery and Fig.221 (lower) in the west doorway at Porchester Priory

king. Therefore, the inclusion of this motif at Leominster may be associated with the patronage of the king.

It is generally accepted that a high vault was originally planned for the nave of Leominster Priory. Whether this was to be a series of domes in the manner of the churches of the Perigord and Angoumois,[8] or a high groin vault in the manner of the nave of Chepstow Priory is a moot point.[9] Be that as it may, there are indicators of inspiration from western France. The carving of the interior of the doorway is paralleled in the south portal at Sainte-Hilaire at Melle.[10] The single west doorway with the large window above recalls the west front of Fontévrault Abbey church,[11] a church planned for a barrel-vaulted nave but built with domes. At Fontévrault the doorway is round-headed rather than pointed as at Leominster, but pointed arches are common in western France as are doorways which combine carved and uncarved orders.

CHAPTER 11

Other Work

FOWNHOPE, ST Mary

Fownhope is recorded in Domesday (29.2) as part of the land of Hugh Donkey. It had two priests and a church with half a hide of land, an indication that it was a minster church.[1]

As at Brinsop and Stretton Sugwas, the tympanum at Fownhope is not *in situ*, being reset inside the church below the west window of the nave. In the centre is a large, frontal, seated figure with a cruciform halo and right hand held away from the body in blessing (fig.222). From behind the head a series of rays curve down to the shoulder. The knees and feet are widely spread and on the lap is a smaller figure also with a cruciform halo and giving a blessing with the right hand, whilst a scroll falls across the legs on the left. To either side of this group there are loosely entwined, two-strand stems with scalloped leaves. In the foliage on the right is a large, winged lion, while on the left there is a bird.

Stylistically there is no problem in associating the tympanum with other works of the Herefordshire School. The hieratic pose and the billowing skirt with box pleats at the hem compare closely with Christ as the Good Shepherd on a capital from St Giles' Hospital, Hereford (fig.184) which, in turn, has been related to voussoir No.13 at the apex of the second order of the right arch at Shobdon. The huge, staring eyes of both Fownhope figures, the foliage, the lion's head and the bird all have close parallels at Kilpeck and elsewhere. But the iconography is not so straightforward. The central group is usually identified as the Virgin and Child, even though the Virgin appears remarkably masculine and has a cruciform halo, an attribute normally reserved for Christ or God the father. The hieratic pose of the Virgin in Majesty has been related to the Byzantine Nikopoios (Victory-Maker) type.[2] By the twelfth century this hieratic grouping enjoyed great popularity in Europe, as on the tympanum of the

Fig.222 The reset tympanum at Fownhope Church

south doorway of the west front of Chartres Cathedral. The Virgin and Child painted on the tympanum inside the west end of the nave at St-Savin-sur-Gartempe, Vienne, is a good parallel for the hieratic pose, and it appears that the St-Savin Virgin also holds a small piece of fruit between the thumb and forefinger of her right hand as at Fownhope (figs.222 & rear cover), probably to identify Christ as the Fruit of Mary's womb.[3] A Virgin and Child tympanum would also be most appropriate for a church dedicated to St Mary, but how are we to account for the cruciform halo for the 'Virgin'? It has been interpreted as a mistake by a sculptor who misunderstood the model[4] — such mistakes are known in Romanesque sculpture, as at Pennington, Lancashire, where the archangel on the tympanum wears a cruciform halo.[5] But perhaps there is no mistake and a representation of the Trinity was intended, the Trinity being completed with the bird on the left of the tympanum or, more likely, with a bird carved on a voussoir above the head of God the Father. God the Father and God the Son appeared on one of the capitals of the presbytery east arch at Hereford Cathedral (fig.134), a work important for the Herefordshire sculptors in providing a model for the pose of Christ on the tympana at Shobdon, St Giles at Hereford and Rowlstone. The Trinity with Christ held on the lap of God the Father appears in the pre-Conquest Harley Psalter, albeit not in a frontal hieratic pose.[6]

A dual meaning for the Fownhope tympanum is a distinct possibility, as with the Ascension/Christ in Majesty on the Shobdon, St Giles at Hereford and Rowlstone tympana or the Trinitarian aspect of the Harrowing of Hell on the Eardisley font. The fusion of imagery may be explained with reference to illustrations at the beginning of St John's Gospel. In the early twelfth-century Bible of Saint-Benigne, Dijon, God the Father is enthroned with God the Son in a disc while an anthropomorphic St John gazes up at the couple in the initial I at the beginning of the gospel.[7] This imagery is related to Isaiah 7.14, 'Therefore the Lord himself shall give you a sign; Behold a Virgin shall conceive, and bear a son, and shall call his name Immanuel.' In the ninth-century Constantinopolitan Khludov Psalter[8], on folio 44, Mary appears as a demi-figure who clasps the shoulders of her son, the Immanuel.[9] Above this group are the dove of the Holy Spirit and the hand of God the Father to indicate that the Virgin's son is the second person of the Trinity. In the Grimbald Gospels,[10] which was produced at Canterbury or Winchester in the early eleventh century, the beginning of St John's Gospel occupies facing pages.[11] In the border above the author portrait on fol. 114v there are three mandorlas, each held by four angels, which enclose a seated figure to represent the Trinity. Opposite, in the upper border of the opening text page, the Virgin and Child are shown in a mandorla supported by four angels. Fusion of the Grimbald Gospel images would result in the central group at Fownhope. The bird refers to St John's Gospel while the winged lion, the symbol of St Mark, suggests specific reference to chapter 16, verse 19, of St Mark's Gospel which tells that the Lord 'was received up into heaven, and sat on the right hand of God.' Therefore, far from being a misunderstood representation of the Virgin and Child, the Fownhope tympanum could be an ingenious combination of Virgin and Child and Trinitarian imagery.

Of the Romanesque fabric of Fownhope church the axial tower survives. Originally it would have stood between the nave and the sanctuary. The arch from the nave to the tower is of two plain orders on scalloped capitals and coursed shafts. The jambs of the chancel arch remain but the arch was replaced in the fourteenth century when the present chancel was built. Beak-spur bases appear on the shafts of the belfry openings where there is also the distinctive volute type of capital of the Dymock School in which there is a raised, stepped pattern beneath the angle volutes. This Dymock School architectural motif is not found in other works of the Herefordshire School and may therefore suggest that Fownhope is an early work of the latter school, that is before 1130. At the top of the corners of the tower there are heads that relate to the work of the Herefordshire School. At the north-west corner is a cowled head with huge eyes with drilled pupils and centrally parted hair combed slickly to the sides, a relation of Kilpeck corbel No.2 (figs.62 & 223). The north-east mask has foliage speading from the corners of the classical-theatrical mouth and is surrounded by a ruff of hair(?) (fig.224). At the south-east angle are two serpents facing each other who bite the tails of their mate's interlaced body (fig.225). At the south-west angle is a humanoid cat's head (fig.226). The

Fig.223 (left) Head at the north-west corner of the tower and
Fig.224 (centre) at the north-east corner of the tower of Fownhope Church
Fig.225 (right) Two serpents at the south-east corner

closest parallel seems to be between the head at the north-west corner of the north nave aisle at Leominster Priory and the north-east and south-west heads at Fownhope. In this connection it may be significant that the top of the

Fownhope tower is finished with a single chevron string course of the same type as on the west front of Leominster. The treatment of the eyes with drilled pupils and scored eyebrow uses the same technique as Kilpeck corbel No.79 (fig.60) although the different shape of the head suggests the work of a different hand.

In 1849 more was preserved. 'Some impaired bases and capitals of Norman pillars, of a size corresponding with the doorway, were, upon the authority of an antiquary who has long resided near the locality, to be seen some years since, as well as some fragments of very early Norman work under the singing-gallery. Two capitals are now preserved and used as flower pots at the Vicarage-house door.'[12]

Fig.226 Humanoid cat's head at the south-west corner of the tower

CHADDESLEY CORBETT, Worcestershire, St Cassian

St Cassian's is an ancient minster church which at Domesday (28.1) was held by Ediva, a woman, from the king, and had two priests with four bordars. Chaddesley Manor contained 25 hides of land and had eight berewicks—outlying parts of the manor. The church was granted to

Fig.227 The font at Chaddesley Corbett Church

Tewkesbury Abbey on 13 September 1114.[13]

The tightly woven, two-strand interlace at the rim, and the angular, two-strand interlace on the splayed foot of the Chaddesley Corbett font repeat those motifs at Eardisley (figs.195 & 227). At Chaddesley Corbett there is a massive interlaced knop rather than the simple cable at Eardisley, and the Chaddesley Corbett font takes on a more pronounced chalice shape than at Eardisley. In this regard it is closer to Castle Frome (figs.187) or the unadorned bowl of the Shobdon font. The carvings again illustrate the sacaments of Baptism and Eucharist.[14] The heads of the five serpentine dragons have been compared with the head of a monster on a pulpit in the abbey of San Giulio on the island of the same name in Lake Orta in Piedmont.[15] A similar formal comparison, but one that is geographically much closer, is with a pre-Conquest(?) loose head at the west end of the nave at Llantwit Major (fig.228). The wildly interlaced bodies of the Chaddesley Corbett dragons are of Anglo-Saxon derivation like the Kilpeck south doorway impost and the panel at Alveley (figs.58 & 163). Needless to say the dragons represent evil forces over which the Christian can triumph through Baptism. The sculpture is of very high quality and the parallels with Kilpeck and Eardisley suggest that if should be attributed to the Chief Master.

Fig.228 Head from Llantwit Major that compares in style with that on the dragon on the Chaddesley Corbett font

Related to the Chaddesley Corbett dragons is one on a south base of the western crossing arch of the Bishop of Lichfield's collegiate church of St Laurence at Gnosall, Staffordshire (fig.229).[16] This is the only aspect of the surviving sculpture at Gnosall that relates to the Herefordshire School, though the triforium in the west wall of the south transept at Gnosall is closely related to those in the nave and transepts at Tewkesbury Abbey, to which Chaddesley Corbett belonged, and a building in which the sculpture is linked to the Herefordshire School. This raises the interesting prospect of the extention of the Herefordshire School into the realm of episcopal patronage in the Lichfield diocese.

Fig.229 A dragon at Gnosall Church, Staffordshire

Framing the tympanum of Christ in Majesty/Ascension on the south doorway of St Kenelm's Chapel, Romsley, Worcestershire, are dragons with interlaced bodies which derive from the

Fig.230 Tympanum above south doorway at Romsley Chapel

Fig.231 Fragment of the tympanum from Chaddesley Corbett reset in the west wall of the west tower

Chaddesley Corbett font (fig.230). The pose of the angels may be inspired by the Herefordshire tympana of the Shobdon Ascension/Christ in Majesty type (fig.126 & 131) but even if this is the case, Romsley stands as a very weak 'copy' of the school—'clearly the product of a rustic imitator.'[17]

A fragment of a tympanum of Christ in Majesty is rebuilt inside the west wall of the tower at Chaddesley Corbett (fig.231) It has been dated earlier than the font and compared with Ribbesford and Romsley,[18] though comparison with the tympanum of the south doorway at Pedmore, Worcestershire, as suggested by Neil Stratford,[19] is far more convincing (fig.232). In particular, there is the beaded mandorla, long, cylindrical toes, box pleats and incised V-folds in the draperies. Neither work is maintream Herefordshire School but other aspects of the Pedmore tympanum suggest that the sculptor knew its works.

Fig.232 The tympanum on the south doorway of Pedmore Church

PEDMORE, Worcestershire, St Peter

The tympanum of the south doorway at Pedmore depicts Christ in Majesty in an oval mandorla which finishes as two grotesque heads beneath His feet surrounded by the four symbols of the evangelists (fig.232). They face in towards Christ in the English manner as at Rochester Cathedral (Zarnecki 1953, ill. 186)—in continental versions of this scene the evangelist symbols move away from the central figure of Christ and turn their heads to look at Him. The beasts trampled beneath the feet of Christ illustrate Psalm 90,[20] while their huge eyes and striated heads are found throughout the Herefordshire School as in the dragon on the Brinsop tympanum (fig.171). The egg-shaped head with large staring eyes of St Matthew in the tympanum relate closely to the Herefordshire type as in the angels on the Rowlstone tympanum, although the Pedmore Matthew is a starched version of the vigorous Rowlstone angels (figs.178). The lion turned *en face* relates to the Shobdon font or the Leominster capitals (fig.150).

Immured in the interior of the north wall of the west tower is a fragment of a cat's mask with the lower half of two beaded medallions issuing from the gaping mouth. Foliage is enclosed in the medallions. The almond-shaped eyes of the mask relate to the outer order of the Kilpeck south doorway. On the left

of the panel there seems to be the upper body of a bird with a large, curled beak, protruding eye, and wing. The lower part of the body cannot be deciphered.

STOTTESDEN, Shropshire, St Mary

Stottesden was an ancient minster church. At Domesday (4.1.30) it was held by Earl Edwin of Earl Roger and by *c.*1138 it may have been a rural deanery of the diocese of Hereford.[23]

The chalice-shaped bowl of the Stottesden font sits on a stem decorated with loosely spiralled, two-strand stems, and

Fig.233 The font at Stottesden Church

Fig.234 (Left) The roundels on Stottesden font are interrupted by an abstract, standing, frontal figure who holds stylized plants to either side of his head. A heavy swag of cloth falls across his lap beneath which a flared skirt extends down to his feet. The ribbed draperies and frontal pose recall the figures on the second pillar of the left arch and second pillar of the chancel arch at Shobdon (details from figs.127 (centre) & 137 (right).

a chamfered base carved with a simple undulating foliage trail (fig.233). Symmetrical three-strand interlace with three-strand roundels at the intersections adorn the rim while on the main section of the bowl are eight beaded roundels joined by grotesque masks and with stylized plants in the spandrels in the manner of the fourth pillar of the chancel arch at Shobdon (figs.140 & 141). To the right of the figure shown in fig.234 is a rosette which is followed by a lion with 'floating' paws who turns his head back to bite his tail exactly like the lion in the third roundel from the bottom on the left of the fourth pillar of the chancel arch at Shobdon (figs.141 & 235). Then comes a griffin turning to peck its neck in the manner of the griffin in the fourth roundel from the bottom on the right of the same Shobdon shaft (figs.141 & 236), followed by an *Agnus Dei*, like the one on the north tympanum at Aston (figs.145 & 233); a quadruped with a dog-like head and lion's body and tail, symmetrical interlace with four angular loops and stylized 'trees' between, similar to the panel to the right of the chancel arch capitals at Rock (figs.155 & 237); four interlacing, two-strand roundels radiating from a small, central boss, exactly as on a panel at Alveley); and finally a large bird with drooping tail pecking the head of a smaller bird with similarities to other work of the school as illustrated. These parallels confirm Zarnecki's attribution of the Stottesden font to the Aston Master.[24]

The large bird with drooping tail pecking the head of a smaller bird from the Stottesden font (top left) with similar work on the fourth pillar of the chancel arch at Shobdon (centre), the north tympanum at Aston (top right), the inner right capital of the chancel arch at Rock (lower left), and the left capital of the north doorway at Ribbesford (lower right)
(details are from figs.234, 140, 146, 155, 158)

At the present state of research it is not possible to suggest a patron for the font, although a date around 1138 in association with the creation of the rural deanery is entirely credible.

BILLESLEY, Warwickshire, All Saints

The tympanum, which was reused as building material in the seventeenth-century wall of the vestry of All Saints, Billesley,[21] shows 'a man pursued by evil forces, personified by a snake and a dragon, and he strives to escape towards a dove, a symbol of purity' (fig.238).[22] There is also a fragment of another tympanum carved with the Harrowing of Hell in which Christ's pose is a blend of those in the same scene at Shobdon and on the Eardisley font (figs.125, 196, 197 & 239). Stylistically the knight is closely related to those

Details from the Stottesden font.

Fig.235 (above left) A lion biting his tail (comparable to a carving at Shobdon);

Fig.236 (top right) A griffin pecking its neck (also comparable to a carving at Shobdon;

Fig.237 (left) Symmetrical interlace with four angular hoops (similar to a carving at Rock)

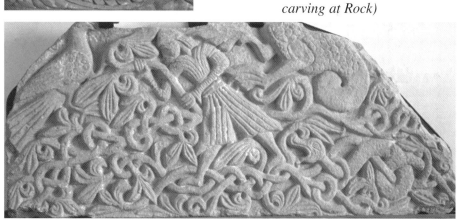

Fig.238 The tympanum at Billesley Church

on the Alveley panel and the Eardisley font (fig.102). The serpent is closest to the capital of the third pillar of the left arch at Shobdon (fig.128), whilst the prancing pose of the dragon goes with the lion of the Eardisley font (fig.198). The foliage belongs to the same stock as that on the panel behind the dragon's head at the south-west angle of the nave at Kilpeck (fig.7).

Presumably the Harrowing of Hell was on the north doorway as at Shobdon, Beckford, Worcestershire, and Quenington, Gloucestershire, whilst the knight was on the south.

Domesday (18.14) lists Billesley on the land of Hugh Grandmesnil of which five hides were held by Osbern and that there were eight villagers and a priest. The present state of research has not revealed clues as to the patron of the sculpture.

LLANBADARN FAWR, Radnorshire, St Padarn

The south doorway of the nave of St Padarn, Llanbadarn Fawr, is an outlier of the Herefordshire School (fig.240). It has two orders of chevron in the arch; the inner order is a double row to either side of a thin roll set at right angles to the wall; the outer order, a flat triple design with chunky little

Fig.239 Fragment of a second tympanum at Billesley Church

triangles in the angle as in the works of the Dymock School (fig.24). The tympanum is truncated; nor does it fill the space laterally. The clean stones above and to the sides of the tympanum are the product of restoration but even with their removal and juggling the placement of the tympanum in the mind's eye do not suggest an alternate setting. In the centre is a sparsely leafed tree which grows from the top of a cat's head. It is possible that the tree originally extended upwards on to another stone in the manner of the Pauntley and Kilpeck tympana (figs.5 & 24). To the left of the cat's head is a disc with an eight-pronged star pattern in the centre. To the right of the tree there is a lion and to the left a quadruped. Both creatures have a tail that passes between their hind legs and above their body to end in a trefoil. Their 'floating' legs, huge eyes and gaping mouths relate them to creatures throughout the Herefordshire School while the 'dog', complete with the trefoil-ended tail, is of the same breed as the one on the panel behind the dragon's head at the south-west corner of the Kilpeck nave (fig.54). The lintel is scored with a joggled pattern and is carried on two corbels originally carved with heads of which only that on the

Fig.240 Tympanum on south doorway at Llanbadarn Fawr

right survives. It is crudely carved and has a long, pencil moustache and a goatee beard. On the right capital a dragon turns to devour a bird while its tail is bitten by a dog(?). The abacus preserves remnants of a chip-carved pattern above a row of balls. On the left capital there is a standing figure on each face and on the right face with a long pony tail. A head is carved at the lower angle. On the abacus there is a dragon with an interlacing body; a weak copy the the Shobdon capitals.

The tympanum is a weak copy of the Herefordshire School. The current state of research has not revealed a patron or date for the work.

THE DEPOSITION IVORY

The ivory relief of the Deposition preserved in the Victoria and Albert Museum[25] has been associated both with the Herefordshire School,[26] and Spain.[27] The form of the heads, the large, bulging eyes and sad expressions, compare favourably with the Kilpeck chancel arch figures amongst others (figs.119-21). The pose of Nicodemus—the figure at bottom right removing a nail from Christ's foot—with body in profile and head turned towards the viewer, is a composite of the St John the Baptist on the Castle Frome font (fig.188), and the figures on the centre capital of the left splay of the west doorway at Leominster Priory (fig.211). The strained juxtaposition of the head and neck of Joseph of Arimathea—the figure clutching Christ's midrif—in the ivory is virtually identical to St John the Baptist on the Castle Frome font (fig.188). The draperies are a more linear version of the tight-fitting garments worn by the Kilpeck chancel arch figures (figs.119-21) and the 'Virgin' on the Fownhope tympanum (fig.222), while the multiple fine folds are paralleled on the cloak of St George on the Brinsop tympanum (fig.171). The striated folds of the garments of the Virgin and St Mary Magdalene relate to the St Michael at Alveley (fig.242). The flared, ribbed trousers of Joseph of Arimathea are

Fig.241 The Deposition ivory, held in the Victoria & Albert Museum London

Comparisons with the carving on the Deposition ivory can be made with (left) Fig.119 St Peter on the Chancel arch at Kilpeck; (above) Fig.188 The figure of John the Baptist on the Castle Frome font; and (right) Fig.242 the garments of St Michael at Alveley

from a similar pattern to those worn by St George at Brinsop, and Samson at Stretton Sugwas, amongst others (figs.167 & 171). The gesture of St Mary Magdalene—at the lower left corner of the ivory—with elongated fingers parallels the 'Virgin' on the Fownhope tympanum (fig.222). The leaves on the latter are of the same genus as on the right and lower borders of the ivory. The foliage trail on the left border with spiralling teminations to individual leaves and binding ties relates closely to the panels behind the dragons' heads at the angles of the nave at Kilpeck (fig.7). The angels are clad in body-hugging clothes but are more angular in pose than their counterparts on the Rowlstone tympanum or the Castle Frome font (figs.178 & 193). The pose, especially the sharply elevated lower legs, reflects an Anglo-Saxon tradition as in the angels at St Lawrence, Bradford-on-Avon, Wiltshire, and St Michael, Winterbourne Steepleton, Dorest.[28] The pose also suits the rectangular frame of the ivory which is not conducive to the flowing poses associated with the semi-circular head of the Rowlstone tympanum. The turn of the head of the left angel towards the viewer reflects the angel on a capital from the east arch of the presbytery at Hereford Cathedral but the heads of the ivory angels have a distinct triangulation and almost a space-alien quality. The simple bold carving of the eyes, nose and mouth, suggests Celtic analogues, and also parallels with five heads reset in the east wall of the south tower of St Mary at Kington. That the Kington heads are twelfth-century is suggested because four are set as two pairs in the manner of those that flank the twelfth-century north doorway at St Mary at Middleton-on-the-Hill.

The closeness of these parallels suggests that the ivory was produced at a centre associated with the Herefordshire School, and possibly in a workshop in Hereford Cathedral itself. More generally, an English provenance is supported by the semi-circular ends to the arms of the cross as in the 'pillow' stones (grave markers) from Hartlepool.[29] However, the Deposition carving is in elephant ivory which is common in Spain yet extremely unusual in England in the twelfth century where walrus ivory or even whalebone were used.[30] The dilemma is not easily resolved. Perhaps Oliver de Merlimond returned from his pilgrimage to Santiago de Compostella with a piece of uncarved elephant ivory.

ADDENDUM to Reprint

ORLETON, St George

Fig. 243 The font at Orleton

Domesday Book (9.19) records that Orleton belonged to Ralph de Mortimer, Lord of Wigmore.

The cylindrical font in the south-west corner of the nave is carved with nine figures each standing under a three-order, round-headed arch set on moulded capitals, half-shafts and cushion bases (fig.243). The moulded capitals relate to those in the nave arcades of the great Romanesque west country abbey churches at Tewkesbury, Gloucester (now cathedral) and Great Malvern. The latter also provides a parallel for the three-order arches. The grooved, cushion bases are the same as those on the west window at Kilpeck (fig.55). The figures are strictly frontal and have large egg-shaped heads with huge, staring eyes, and big hands, when open, like the figures on the Kilpeck chancel arch (figs.119-122). However, the figures lack the high quality of the work at Kilpeck or the fonts by the Chief Master of the Herefordshire School at Eardisley and Castle Frome (figs.187 & 195). These fonts also differ from Orleton in their chalice shape. All the figures on the Orleton font carry books in the left hand and St Peter is identified by the keys held in his right hand. Some figures appear to carry candles and as such relate to some of the figures reset above the vestry door at Brinsop (fig.175).

A fragmentary carved shaft, illustrated in volume III of the *Royal Commission on Historical Monuments, Herefordshire*, pl.16, recently reappeared in the crypt of Hereford Cathedral when the cases from the former exhibition in the treasury were dismantled. The Royal Commission (p.157) describes the shaft as 'a mutilated stone, formerly used as a clock weight' 18 inches in length. The shaft was formerly at Orleton church until the late 1940s when, on the advice of Professor George Zarnecki, and the permission of the incumbent of Orleton, the shaft was moved to the cathedral for safe keeping. It has now been restored to Orleton. On the right of the shaft there is a dragon; the striated head with large eye, gaping mouth and flared lips, top of the leg and beginning of the wing are still relatively clear. The dragon is about to bite a twisting, heavily scaled serpent or tail of another dragon. Stylistically the fragment belongs to the Herefordshire School. Shafts carved with serpents occur on the south doorway at Kilpeck and with dragons on the fifth pillar of the chancel arch at Shobdon (fig.142). The scaly body is allied to corbel no.4 at Kilpeck, to various examples at Shobdon, and to the dragon on the St George tympanum at Brinsop (figs.64, 128, 132 & 171). The head of the Brinsop dragon also relates closely to the Orleton dragon. Originally, the Orleton shaft would have adorned the chancel arch or a doorway to the church. Like the fragmentary carved shaft at Eardisley, the Orleton stone shows that the 12th-century church was originally decorated more completely with sculpture of the Herefordshire School.

In spite of its poor condition the Orleton shaft, unlike the font, seems once to have been a top quality work. For this it is likely that we are dealing with the patronage of Hugh de Mortimer and his chief steward, Oliver de Merlimond. It is possible that the poorer quality of the sculpture of the Orleton font suggests that it was executed after 1143 when Oliver had left the employ of Hugh de Wigmore at which time his advice on artistic matters was no longer available to Hugh.

EDVIN LOACH, St Mary (Old Church)

Fig. 244 Part of the font at Edvin Loach

Five fragments of a cylindrical font from the Romanesque church of St Mary at Edvin Loach are preserved in the English Heritage stone store at Atcham (Shropshire). Four of the pieces (cat.88108509) are carved with simple chevron like that on the west front of Monmouth priory (fig.206). The fifth stone (cat.880603) is adorned with five circular medallions joined with binding ties and is rather worn (fig.244). Birds inhabit the first and third medallions. They extend their heads beyond outside the medallion to peck the intermediate medallion in which there is a quadruped(?). A four-lobed leaf fills the fourth medallion, and in the fifth medallion there is a raised roundel with fluted sides. Above the medallions are grooved stems which may have formed larger medallions. The inhabited medallions are generally allied to this motif elsewhere in the Herefordshire School but most closely to the sixth pillar of the Shobdon chancel arch on which birds extend their head outside the medallions (fig.144).

Research to date has not provided clues as to the patron of the Edvin Loach font.

Illustrated Glossary for some of the architectural/ornamental terms used in the text

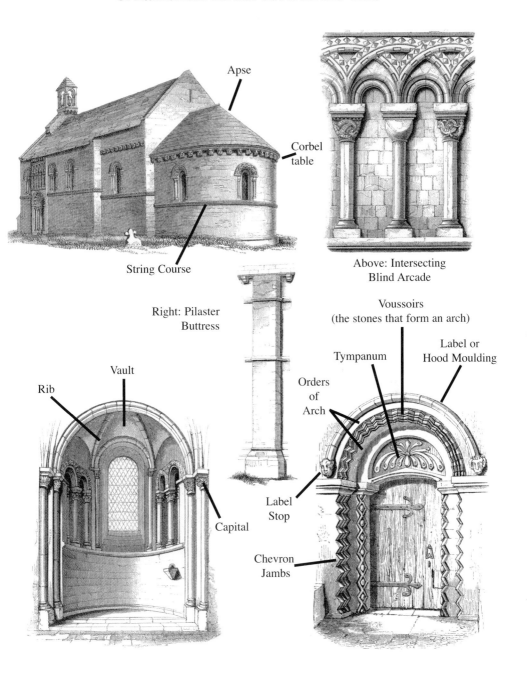

Apse

Corbel table

String Course

Above: Intersecting Blind Arcade

Right: Pilaster Buttress

Voussoirs
(the stones that form an arch)

Tympanum

Label or Hood Moulding

Orders of Arch

Vault

Rib

Label Stop

Capital

Chevron Jambs

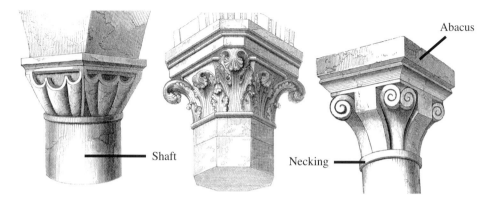

Above: Capitals showing different styles. From left to right: Scalloped, Acanthus, Volute

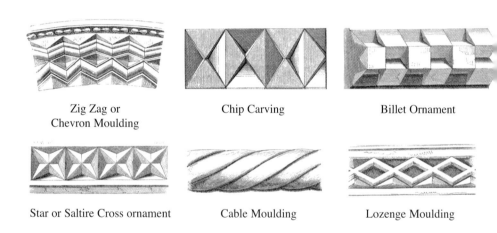

Zig Zag or Chevron Moulding

Chip Carving

Billet Ornament

Star or Saltire Cross ornament

Cable Moulding

Lozenge Moulding

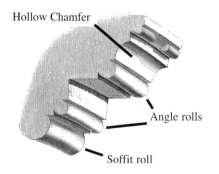

Other terms used:

Foliated: Carved with leaf ornament

Impost: Bracket in a wall, usually formed of mouldings, on which the ends of an arch rest

Nook-shaft: Shaft set in the angle of a pier, respond or wall, or the angle of the jamb of a window or doorway

Respond: A half-pier or half-pillar bonded into a wall and carrying one end of an arch

Stilted arch: An arch with its springing line raised above the level of the imposts

160

ENDNOTES

(For full references refer to the Bibliography)

Introduction
1. Zarnecki 1951b
2. Clanchy1983, 177
3. Wood 1985
4. West 1988
5. Hamer, 20-21
6. Zarnecki 1993

Chapter 1
1. Gem 1980; Fernie 1987
2. Brown 1982, 13
3. Walker 1967-69
4. Shoesmith 1991
5. Wightman 1966
6. Hopkinson 1989
7. Brown 1982, 13
8. Thurlby 1997
9. Gem 1983
10. Fernie 1979
11. Thurlby 1994a
12. Gem 1983, 10
13. Gem 1986, 87
14. Drinkwater 1954 & 1955; Gem 1986
15. Boker 1998
16. Bandmann 1965; Gem 1986, 88; Boker
    1998, 49-50
17. Krautheimer 1986, 356-8; Boker 1998,
    51-2
18. Thurlby 1995a
19. RCHM, I, 92-5
20. Gem 1986, pl. XXIX; Thurlby 1995a,
    pl. IIC
21. Whitehead 1995
22. Brown 1982, 13
23. Binns 1989, 75
24. Dimock, VI, 40; Wightman 1966, 183
25. Wightman 1966, 175
26. Lloyd 1912, 443
27. Green 1986, 253
28. Ibid, 252-3
29. Dimock, VI, 34
30. Walker 1958, 69-70
31. RRAN, II, No.1280
32. Walker 1960, 186-8
33. Walker 1958, 70
34. Potter 1976, 24/25
35. RRAN, II, 424; Wightman 1966, 175, 178;

Hollister 1986, 241
36. CDF, No.288, No.609, No.610 and
    No.1389
37. CDF No.609, No.610, No,1389 and
    RRAN, II, No.1261
38. CDF No.609, No.610, No.1389
39. RRAN, II, No.1041
40. Patterson 1973, No.96
41. Walker 1964, No.48
42. Dickinson & Ricketts, 423
43. RRAN, II, 437
44. Wharton 1691, II, 300
45. Hart 1863, 73

Chapter 2
1. Pevsner 1963, 202
2. Boase 1953, 84
3. cf. Heslop 1985
4. Barber 1993, 7-9; Baxter 1998
5. Oxford, Bodleian Library MS laud. Misc.
    247 S.C. 1302
6. Bodleian MS Bodley 764
7. Baxter 1998, 160
8. Kendrick 1949, 140-1
9. Thurlby 1996
10. Whitehead 1995
11. RCHM, I, pl.149
12. Hereford Cathedral MS P.4.III, fol.3;
    Boase, pl.22a & b
13. Chwojko & Thurlby 1997, pls.IIIA & D
14. Ibid, pls.IVA & B
15. Kunstler 1973, pl.222
16. Thurlby 1985
17. Chwojko & Thurlby 1997, 18
18. Welander 1991, 82
19. Chwojko & Thurlby 1997, pls.VA & B
20. Welander 1991, 63
21. Thurlby 1980
22. Ibid, 93
23. cat. 79/1C
24. Borg 1985
25. Prior & Gardner 1912
26. Stone 1955, 69
27. VCH, Gloucestershire, VIII, 199
28. King 1995; Thurlby 1995
29. Brandon & Brandon 1858, pl.4
30. Welander 1991, 55

31. Chwojko & Thurlby 1997, fig.1
32. Keyser 1927, fig.117
33. Zarnecki 1951b, 294
34. Chwojko & Thurlby 1997, VIID;
    Gethyn-Jones 1979, pl.48a
35. Gethyn-Jones 1979, pl.35e
36. Taylor & Taylor 1965, 222
37. RCAHM Glamorgan, 61-2, cat.938
38. Hauglid 1973; Hohler 1979
39. British Museum, MLA 1960, 7-1, 1
40. Gem 1995, 47-8
41. Speake 1980, 21, fig.5
42. Whitfield 1993, fig.14.1
43. Hinton 1974, 55
44. Evans 1986, pls.VII & VIII
45. Wilson 1984, pl.62
46. Kendrick 1949, pl.LXXXI
47. Megaw 1970, ill.209
48. Toynbee 1964, 56
49. Greene 1975; Henig 1993, 78
50. Hearn 1981, pls.102 & 106
51. Pevsner 1963, 203
52. Zarnecki 1997
53. Porter 1917, II, 407
54. Zarnecki 1951b; 1953; Stone 1955, 67
55. Jonsdottir 1950
56. Stone 1955, 2243 n.4
57. Zarnecki *et al* 1984, 174, cat. 129
58. Ibid, 171, cat. 127s
59. Zarnecki 1951b
60. RRAN, II, No.1723
61. Zarnecki et al 1984, 174, cat. 129
62. Halsey 1985
63. King 1995, 86-7
64. Ibid, 86
65. Ibid, 86
66. n. A.4-1946
67. Williamson 1983, 88
68. King 1995, 85
69. King 1990, 79
70. Stalley 1971, 71
71. Thurlby 1982b, 96-7

Chapter 3
1. Harvey 1987, 27
2. Ibid, 254
3. Ibid, 152
4. Barrow, 45, n.46
5. Zarnecki 1951b

6. Zarnecki 1953, 14
7. Eygun 1970, 179
8. Willis 1845, 59
9. Thurlby 1995; Williamson 1995, 4-6
10. Jonsdottir 1950; Stone 1955
11. Stone 1955, 69
12. Kendrick 1936
13. Cambridge, Corpus Christi College, MS 2
14. Kauffmann 1966, 63-4

Chapter 4
1. Pevsner 1963, 201
2. Shoesmith 1992, 162
3. Heslop 1994
4. Hart 1863, 16
5. VCH Herefordshire, I, 358-9
6. Toynbee and Ward Perkins 1956;
    Thurlby 1994a
7. Thurlby 1994a
8. Thurlby 1988; 1994a; 1994b
9. Gethyn-Jones 1979, pl.60a & b
10. Fernie 1992
11. Shoesmith 1992, 202
12. King 1995, 82-3
13. Ibid, 82
14. Ibid, 83
15. Keyser 1927, xxxvii
16. Barber 1993, 180-1
17. cf. Heslop 1985, 8-9
18. Hamer
19. Ibid
20. Anon 1989, 3
21. Barber 1993, 142
22. Ibid, 183
23. White 1960, 51
24. Barber 1993, 26
25. Ibid 173
26. Ibid 118-9
27. Ibid 136
28. Pevsner 1963, 202
29. Anon 1989, 330.
30. Barber 1993, 147
31. Ibid 166-8
32. Ibid 177
33. Ibid 79-80
34. Ibid 84
35. Ibid 86
36. Ibid 83
37. Ibid 44; White 1960, 29

38. Ibid 45
39. Grandsen 1972
40. Barber 1993, 72
41. Ibid 66
42. Weir and Jerman 1986, 100-5
43. Barber 1993, 51-2
44. Ibid 83
45. Lewis 1842, XViii
46. Hamer
47. Boase 82

Chapter 5
1. Dickinson and Ricketts, 423-5
2. Zarnecki 1997
3. Zarnecki 1993, 88
4. Ibid, 87
5. Hamer
6. Keyser 1927, figs.95 & 97; Zarnecki 1994
7. Hamer
8. Zarnecki 1951b, 267; Goldschmidt & Weitzmann 1979, No.115
9. Goldschmidt I, No.185
10. Zarnecki 1951b, 268
11. British Library, Harley MS 603
12. Kalinowski 1993
13. Backhouse *et al* 1984, cat. 129
14. Zarnecki 1997, 105
15. British library, Cotton MS Nero D IV; Backhouse 1981
16. Stalley 1996
17. Nash-Williams
18. Pevsner 1963, 288
19. Bond 1908, 110
20. Barber 24-5
21. Krautheimer 1942; Thurlby 1982a
22. Zarnecki et al 1984, cat. 172s
23. Wharton 1691, 299-300
24. Zarnecki 1994, 214

Chapter 6
1. Zarnecki 1953, 14
2. Gethyn-Jones, pls.9-11
3. Sauerlander 1992, 19
4. Gethyn-Jones, pl.60a
5. Ibid, pls.59 & 60
6. Kendrick 1949, pl.LII; Zarnecki 1951b, 230
7. Meredith 1980, 335; Zarnecki 1997, 102
8. RCHM, III, xxviii
9. Tonkin 1982, 32

10. VCH Worcester IV, 320
11. Bond 1988, 140
12. Zarnecki 1990
13. Allen 1887, ill. opp. 347
14. Barber, 204
15. Zarnecki 1953, 14
16. VCH Worcester, IV, 306
17. Bond 1988, figs.36-40
18. Zarnecki 1978, pl.IIIB
19. Pevsner 1968, 249
20. Zarnecki 1951b, 229
21. VCH Shropshire, II, 123-8; Clark-Maxwell & Thompson 1927, 4
22. RRAN, III, No.437
23. Hunt & Stokes 1997
24. Zarnecki 1990
25. Hunt & Stokes, pl.IXA & B
26. Kahn 1991
27. Zarnecki 1978
28. Hunt and Stokes 1997, 31-2
29. Bayle 1992
30. Kahn 1992
31. Jewell 1986
32. Banks 1883, 141-2
33. RRAN, II, No.1280
34. Dickinson & Ricketts, 425
35. Banks 1883, 147
36. Focillon 1963, 105-12
37. Zarnecki 1953, 13, 55
38. Zarnecki 1994
39. Vermasaren 1963; Ulansey 1989
40. Andreae 1978, pl.106
41. Ibid, pl.105
42. Ulansey 1989, pl.2.1
43. Toynbee 1962, cat. 69, pl.73
44. Zarnecki 1997, 94; Brewer 1986, 35-6, pl.19
45. Henig 1993, cat. 137 & 140
46. Huskisson 1994, 16
47. Webster, pls.XVIII, XX
48. Zarnecki 1951b, 336
49. Ibid, 324
50. Zarnecki 1994, 214
51. Hamer; RCHM II, 31-2

Chapter 7
1. Wightman 1966
2. Giraldus Cambrensis VI, 34
3. Roberts 1846, 236

4. Blashill 1891, 249
5. RCHM, I, pl.8
6. Oursel 1984, pls.130 & 131
7. Hearn & Thurlby, 54-5
8. Renn 1961
9. Brown 1954, 78
10. Thurlby 1995, pl.IC
11. Lloyd 1912, 443
12. Walker 1964, No.18
13. RCHM, I, 131
14. Pevsner 1963, 185
15. RRAN, II, 308
16. Round 1888, No.21
17. RCHM, II, 49
18. Pevsner 1963, 99
19. Thurlby 1984
20. Thurlby 1995
21. Zarnecki et al 1984, cat. 139
22. Krautheimer 1942
23. RCHM, I, 92-5
24. Zarnecki 1951b, 316
25. RCHM, II, pl.54

Chapter 8
1. Holtzmann 1930, No.26
2. Walker 1964, No.2
3. Copplestone-Crow, 19
4. Nash-Williams, cat. 221
5. Zarnecki 1997, 107
6. Copplestone-Crow, 20
7. Kaske 1988, 186
8. Krautheimer 1942
9. Thurlby 1982a
10. Thurlby 1980
11. RCHM, II, 52
12. Tonkin 1982, 33
13. Zarnecki 1953, 12-3, 55
14. Ibid, 9-10, 12-3
15. Gethyn-Jones, pl.12

Chapter 9
1. CDF No.1133; Binns 1989, 106
2. CDF No.1138
3. CDF No.1142
4. CDF, 406-14
5. Morris 1983, 201
6. Gethyn-Jones, pl.39b
7. CDF, No.1133
8. CDF, No.1136

9. RCHM, I, 74; Radford 1958, 5
10. CDF, No.1142

Chapter 10
1. RCHM, III, plan opp. 111
2. Thurlby 1995b
3. Gethyn-Jones, pl.47c
4. Ibid, pl.32
5. King 1986, 27
6. Halsey 185; Brooke 1993; Thurlby 1995c, 793-6
7. Smith 1963
8. Thurlby 195, 23-4
9. Oursel 1984, pl.116; Zarnecki 1997, 100
10. Zarnecki 1997, 100

Chapter 11
1. Blair 1985
2. Zarnecki 1951b, 339
3. Heslop 1978, 75-6
4. Boase 1953, 83
5. Zarnecki 1951b, 339; Keyser 1927, fig.137
6. British Library Harley MS 603, fol.1; Temple, ill.210
7. Schiller 1972, 6-7, fig.1
8. Moscow, Historical Museum, Cod. Gr. 129
9. Schiller 1972, 7, fig.3
10. British Library MS Add. 34890
11. Fols.114v and 115
12. Anon. 1849, 80
13. RRAN, II, No.1069
14. Thurlby 1982a
15. Zarnecki 1990, 190, fig.3
16. VCH Staffs., IV, 113
17. Zarnecki 1990, 202
18. Roper 1978, 7
19. Pevsner 1968, 117
20. Stratford 1968, 234
21. VCH Warwick, I, 326
22. Zarnecki 1984, 177
23. VCH Shropshire, II, 3
24. Zarnecki 1951b, 318-20; 1953, 14
25. 3-1872
26. Beckwith 1956; 1972, cat. 50
27. Goldschmidt 1926, no.102; Longhurst 1927, 93
28. Wilson 1984, ills.253-5
29. Brown 1921, pl.6
30. Williamson 1982, 16-7

BIBLIOGRAPHY

Abbreviations

AASR&P - *Associated Architectural Societies Reports and Papers*
Antiq. J. - *Antiquaries Journal*
Archaeol. J. - *Archaeological Journal*
Arch. Camb. - *Archaeologia Cambrensis*
BAA CT - *British Archaeological Association Conference Transactions*
Burl. Mag. - *Burlington Magazine*
CDF - *Calendar of Documents preserved in France illustrative of the History of Great Britain and Ireland, I, AD 918-1206*, ed. J. Horace Round, London, 1899
DB - *Domesday Book*
Gent's Mag. - *The Gentleman's Magazine*
JBAA - *Journal of the British Archaeological Association*
JSAH - *Journal of the Society of Architectural Historians*
JWCI - *Journal of the Warburg and Courtauld Institutes*
RCAHM Glamorgan - *Royal Commission on Ancient and Historical Monuments in Wales. Inventory of the Ancient Monuments in Glamorgan, I, Pre-Norman, Part III, The Early Christian Period*, Cardiff 1976
RCHM *Herefordshire - I, South-West*, London, 1931; *II, East*, London, 1932; *III, North-West*, London, 1934
RRAN - *Regesta Regum Anglo-Normanorum 1066-1154, II, Regesta Henrici Primi, 1100-1135*, ed. Charles Johnson and H.A. Cronne, London, 1956
TBGAS - *Transactions of the Bristol and Gloucestershire Archaeological Society*
TWNFC - *Transactions of the Woolhope Naturalists' Field Club*
VCH - *The Victoria History of the Counties of England*
WANHM - *Wiltshire Archaeological and Natural History Magazine*

Addyman, P. & Morris, R. (eds.) 1976. *The Archaeological Study of Churches*. Council for British Archaeology Report No. 13.
Allen, J.R. 1887. 'Norman Sculpture and the Medieval Bestiaries', in *Early Christian Symbolism in Great Britain and Ireland*. London (reprinted Llanarch, n.d.).
Allen, J. R. 1906. 'Early Christian Art: Norman Sculpture', *VCH Worcester*, II, 189-95.
Andersen, J. 1977. *The Witch on the Wall*. London.
Andreae, B. 1978. *The Art of Rome*. London.
Anon., 1843. [Kilpeck Church] 'A Gem of the Norman Era', *The Builder*, I, 277.
Anon., 1849. 'Fownhope Church, Herefordshire', *The Builder*, VII, 80.
Anon., 1989. *Guide to the Parish Church of SS. Mary & David, Kilpeck*.
Backhouse, J. 1981. *The Lindisfarne Gospels*. London.
Backhouse, J.; Turner, D.H. and Webster, L., (eds.) 1984. *The Golden Age of Anglo-Saxon Art 966-1066*. London.
Bandmann, D. 1965. 'Die Bischofskapelle in Hereford', in *Festschrift fur Herbert von Einem*, Berlin, 9-26.
Banks, R.W. (ed.) 1882. 'Cartularium Prioratus S. Johannis Evang. de Brecon', *Arch. Camb.*, XIII, 275-308.
Banks, R.W. (ed.) 1883. 'Cartularium Prioratus S. Johannis Evang. de Brecon', *Arch. Camb.*, XIV, 18-49, 137-68, 221-36 and 274-311.

Bannister, A.T. 1902-4. 'The Hereford Domesday', *TWNFC*, 318-25.

Barber, R. 1993. *Bestiary: Being An English Version of the Bodleian Library, Oxford, MS Bodley 764*. Woodbridge.

Barlow, F. 1979. *The English Church 1066-1154*. London and New York.

Barrow, J. 1995. 'A Lotharingian in Hereford: Bishop Robert's Reorganization of the Church of Hereford 1079-1095', *BAA CT*, XV, 29-29.

Bayle, M. 1992. 'Frises et dalles sculptée dans l'architecture romane en Normandie', in Kahn 1992a. 75-83.

Bayle, M. (ed.) (1997). *L'architecture normande au Moyen Age*. Caen.

Baxter, R. (1998). *Bestiaries and their users in the Middle Ages*. Stroud.

Beckwith, J. 1956. 'An Ivory Relief of the Deposition', *Burl. Mag.*, XCVIII, 228-35.

Beckwith, J. 1972. *Ivory Carvings in Early Medieval England*. London.

Binns, A. 1989. *Dedications of Monastic Houses in England and Wales 1066-1216*. Woodbridge.

Blair, J. 1985. 'Secular Minster Churches in Domesday Book', in *Domesday Book: A Reassessment*, ed. Peter Sawyer, London, 104-42.

Blair, J. (ed.). 1988a. *Minsters and Parish Churches: The Local Church in Transition*. Oxford.

Blair, J. 1988b. 'Introduction: from Minster to Parish Church', in Blair 1988a, 1-20.

Blashill, T. 1871. 'On the Churches of Kilpeck and Rowlstone', *JBAA*, XXVII, 489-95.

Blashill, T. 1890-2. 'Rowlstone Church', *TWNFC*, 249-50.

Boase, T.S.R. 1953. *English Art 1100-1216*. Oxford.

Boker, H. 1998. 'The Bishop's Chapel of Hereford Cathedral and the Question of Architectural Copies in the Middle Ages', *Gesta*, XXXVII/1, 44-54.

Bond,C.J. 1988. 'Church and Parish in Norman Worcestershire', in Blair 1988a, 119-58.

Bond, F. 1908. *Fonts and Font Covers*. London.

Bony, J. 1958. 'La chapelle episcopale de Hereford et les apports lorrains en Angleterre après la conquete', in *Actes du XIXe congres international d'histoire de l'art*. Paris, 36-43.

Borg, A. 1985. 'The Gloucester Candlestic', *BAA CT*, VII, 84-92.

Brandon, R. & Brandon, J.A. 1858. *An Analysis of Gothic Architecture*, II. London.

Brewer, R.J. 1986. *Corpus Signorum Imperii Romani. Great Britain, I, Fascicule 5,Wales*. Oxford.

Brooke, C. 1993. 'Bishop Walkelin and his inheritance', in *Winchester Cathedral: Nine Hundred Years*, ed. J. Crook, Chichester, 1-12.

Brown, G.B. 1921. *The Arts in Early England*, V. London.

Brown, R.A. 1954. *English Castles*. London.

Brown, R.A. 1982. 'William of Malmesbury as an architectural historian', in *Melanges d'archeologie et d'histoitre medievales en l'honeur de Doyen Michel de Bouard* (Memoires et documents publies par la societe de l'ecole de Chartes, XXVII), Geneva, 9-16, reprinted in R.A. Brown, *Castles, Conquest and Charters*. Woodbridge, 1989, 227-34.

Buckingham, C.S. 1908. 'Kilpeck and its Church', *JBAA*, N.S. XIV, 73-82.

Buckton, D. & Heslop, T.A. (eds.) 1994. *Studies in Medieval Art and Architecture presented to Peter Lasko*. Stroud.

Clapham, A.W. 1930. *English Romanesque Architecture before the Conquest*. Oxford.

Clapham, A.W. 1934a. *English Romanesque Architecture after the Conquest*. Oxford.

Clapham, A.W. 1934b. 'Early Castles in Herefordshire', *RCHM Herefordshire*, III, lxii-lxiii.

Chwojko, E. & Thurlby, M. 1997. 'Gloucester and the Herefordshire School', *JBAA*, CL, 7-26.

BIBLIOGRAPHY

Clanchy, M.T. 1983. *England and its Rulers 1066-1272*. Oxford.

Clark-Maxwell, W.G. & Thompson, A.H. 1927. 'The College of St Mary Magdalene, Bridgnorth, with some Account of its Deans and Prebendaries', *Archaeol. J.*, 2nd ser. XXXIV, 1-87.

Coldstream, N. 1991. *Medieval Craftsmen: Masons and Sculptors*. London.

Coplestone-Crow, B. 1979. 'The Baskervilles of Herefordshire 1086-1300', *TWNFC*, XLIII, 18-39.

Cramp, R. 1977. 'Schools of Mercian Sculpture', in *Mercian Studies*, ed A. Dornier, Leicester, 191-233.

Croom, J. 1988. 'The Fragmentation of the Minster *Parochiae* in South-East Shropshire', in Blair 1988a, 67-81.

Crozet, R. 1971. *L'art roman en Saintonge*. Paris.

Cust, L. 1915-17. 'Kilpeck Church', *Walpole Society*, V. 85-89.

Dickinson, J.C. & Ricketts, P.T. (eds.) 1969. 'The Anglo-Norman Chronicle of Wigmore Abbey', *TWNFC*, 39, 413-46.

Dimock, J.F. (ed.) *Giraldus Cambrensis Opera* (Rolls Series).

Dodwell, C.R. 1982. *Anglo-Saxon Art: A New Perspective*. Ithaca, N.Y.

Domesday Book, Hampshire, ed. J. Munby, Chichester, 1982.

Domesday Book, Herefordshire, ed. F. & C. Thorn, Chichester, 1982.

Domesday Book, Kent, ed. P. Morgan, Chichester, 1983.

Domesday Book, Shropshire, ed. F. & C. Thorn, Chichester, 1986.

Domesday Book, Staffordshire, ed. J. Morris, Chichester, 1976.

Domesday Book, Warwickshire, ed. J. Morris, Chichester, 1976.

Drinkwater, N. 1954. 'Hereford Cathedral, The Bishop's Chapel', *Archaeol. J.*, CXI, 129-37.

Drinkwater, N. 1955. 'Hereford Cathedral, The Bishop's Chapel', *Archaeol. J.*, CXII, 74-75.

Evans, A.C. 1986. *The Sutton Hoo Ship Burial*. London.

Fairholt, F.W. 1846. 'Kilpeck Church, Herefordshire', *The Builder*, IV, 594.

Fairweather, F.H. 1933. *Aisleless Apsidal Churches of Great Britain*. Colchester.

Fernie, E.C. 1985. 'The Effect of the Conquest on Norman Architectural Patronage', *Anglo-Norman Studies*, XI, 71-85.

Fernie, E.C. 1987. 'Reconstructing Edward's Abbey at Westminster', in *Romanesque and Gothic Essays for George Zarnecki*, ed. N. Stratford. Woodbridge, 63-67.

Fernie, E.C. 1992. 'Copford, St Michael and All Angels', *The Colchester Area: Proceedings of the 138th Summer Meeting of the Royal Archaeological Institute*, 28-30.

Fernie, E.C. 1993. 'Design principles of early medieval architecture as exemplified at Durham Cathedral', in *Engineering a Cathedral*, ed. M.J. Jackson. London, 146-55.

Fernie, E.C. 1994. 'Architecture and the Effects of the Norman Conquest', in *England and Normandy in the Middle Ages*, ed. D. Bates & A. Curry. London & Rio Grande, 105-16.

Firmstone, E.R. 1886-9. 'Kilpeck Church', *TWNFC*, 137-39.

Focillon, H. 1963. *The Art of the West: Romanesque*. London.

Gardner, A. 1935. *A Handbook of English Medieval Sculpture*. Cambridge.

Gardner, I. 1927. 'The Church of Kilpeck, Herefordshire', *Arch. Camb.*, 82, 365-77.

Gem, R. 1980. 'The Romanesque Rebuilding of Westminster Abbey', *Proceedings of the Battle Conference*, III, 33-60.

Gem, R. 1983. 'The Romanesque Cathedral of Winchester: Patron and Design', *BAA CT*, VI, 1-12.

Gem, R. 1986. 'The Bishop's Chapel at Hereford: the Roles of Patron and Craftsman', in Macready & Thompson, 87-96.

Gem, R. 1988. 'The English Parish Church in the 11th and Early 12th Centuries: A Great Rebuilding?', in Blair 1988a, 21-30.

Gem, 1995. 'Staged Timber Spires in Carolingian North-East France and Anglo-Saxon England', *JBAA*, CXLVII, 29-54.

Gethyn-Jones, E. 1979. *The Dymock School of Sculpture*. London and Chichester.

Goldschmidt, A. 1918. *Die Elfenbeinskulpturen aus der Zeit der karolingischen und sachischen Kaiser*, IV. Berlin.

Goldschmidt, A. & Weitzmann, K. 1979. *Die byzantinischen Elfenbeinskulpturen des X -XIII Jahrhundert*, II. Berlin.

Gransden, A. 1972. 'Realistic Observation in Twelfth-Century England', *Speculum*, 47, 29-51, reprinted in idem, *Legends, Traditions and History in Medieval England*. London, 1992.

Green, J.A. 1986. *The Government of England under Henry I*. Cambridge.

Greene, K.T. 1975. 'The Romano-Celtic Head from the Bon Marché Site, Gloucester: A Reappraisal', *Antiq. J.*, 55, 338-45.

Halsey, R. 1985. 'Tewkesbury Abbey: some recent observations', *BAA CT*, VII, 16-35.

Hamer, E.R. 1992. 'Patronage and iconography in Romanesque England: The Herefordshire School in Context', unpublished Ph.D. dissertation, University of Chicago.

Harper-Bill, C. 1979. 'The Piety of the Anglo-Norman Knightly Class', *Proceedings of the Battle Conference on Anglo-Norman Studies*, II, 63-77.

Harvey, J. 1987. *English Medieval Architects: A Bibliographical Dictionary down to 1550*. Gloucester.

Haslam, R. 1979. *The Buildings of Wales, Powys*. Harmondsworth.

Harris, A. 1964. 'A Romanesque Candlestick in London', *JBAA*, XXVII, 32-52.

Hart, W.H. (ed.) 1863. *Historia et Cartularium Monasterii Sancti Petri Gloucestriae*, I, Rolls Series. London.

Hart, W.H. (ed.) 1867. *Historia et Cartularium Monasterii Sancti Petri Gloucestriae*, III, Rolls Series. London.

Hearn, M.F. *Romanesque Sculpture*. Ithaca, N.Y.

Hearn, M.F. & Thurlby, M. 1997. 'Previously Undetected Wooden Ribbed Vaults in British Medieval Architecture', *JBAA*, CL, 48-58.

Henig, M. 1993. *Roman Sculpture from the Cotswold Region. Corpus Signorum Imperii*, 1.7. Oxford.

Henig, M. 1995. *The Art of Roman Britain*. London.

Henry, F. & Zarnecki, G. 1957-8. 'Romanesque Arches Decorated with Human and Animal Heads', *JBAA*, 3rd ser. XXI-XXII, 1-35.

Heslop, T.A. 1978. 'The Romanesque Seal of Worcester Cathedral', *BAA CT*, I, 71-79.

Heslop, T.A. 1980. 'English Seals from the mid ninth century to 1100', *JBAA*, CXXXIII, 1-16.

Heslop, T.A. 1984. 'Seals', in Zarnecki *et al*, 298-319.

Heslop, T.A. 1986. 'Brief in words but heavy in the weight of its mysteries', *Art History*, 9, No. 1, 1-11.

Hillaby, J. 1980. 'The Saint that never slept: Robert de Bethune, Bishop of Hereford, 1131-1148', *The Friends of Hereford Cathedral 46th Annual Report*, 21-42.

Hillaby, J. 1993. *The Sculptured Capitals of Leominster Priory*. Leominster.

Hills, G.M. 1871. 'The Architectural History of Hereford Cathedral', *JBAA*, XXVII, 46-84, 496-513.

Hinton, D. 1974. *A Catalogue of the Anglo-Saxon Ornamental Metalwork in the Department of Antiquities, Ashmolean Museum*. Oxford.

Hohler, E.B. 1989. 'Norwegian Stave Church Carving: An Introduction', *Arte Medievale*, 2nd ser. Anno 3, no. 1, 77-116.

Hollister, C.W. 1986. *Monarchy, Magnates and Institutions in the Anglo-Norman World*. London & Ronceverte.

Holtzmann, W. 1930. *Papsturkunden in England*. Berlin.

Hopkinson, C. 1989. 'The Mortimers of Wigmore 1086-1214', *TWNFC*, XLVI, 177-93.

Hunt, J. & Stokes, M.A. 1997. 'Sculpture and Patronage in a Shropshire Manor: A Group of 12th-century Sculptures from Alveley', *JBAA*, CL, 27-47.

Hunter-Blair, C.H. 1943. 'Armorials upon English Seals from the Twelfth to the Sixteenth Century', *Archaeologia*, LXXXIX, 1-26.

Huskinson, J. 1994. *Roman Sculpture from Eastern England. Corpus Signorum Imperii*, 1.8. Oxford.

Jewell, R.H.I. 1986. 'The Anglo-Saxon Friezes at Breedon-on-the-Hill, Leicestershire', *Archaeologia*, 108, 95-115

Jonsdottir, S. 1950. 'The Portal of Kilpeck Church: Its Place in English Romanesque Sculpture', *Art Bulletin*, XXXII, 171-80.

Kahn, D. 1988. 'La sculpture romane en Angleterre: état des questions', *Bulletin Monumental*, 146, 307-40.

Kahn, D. 1991. *Canterbury Cathedral and its Romanesque Sculpture*. Austin, Texas.

Kahn, D. (ed.) 1992a. *The Romanesque Frieze and its Spectator*. London.

Kahn, D. 1992b. 'Anglo-Saxon and Early Romanesque Frieze Sculpture in England', in Kahn 1992a, 61-74.

Kalinowski, L. 1992. 'The "Frieze" at Malmesbury', in Kahn 1992a, 85-96.

Kaske, R.E. 1988. 'Piers Plowman and Local Iconography: The Font at Eardisley, Herefordshire', *JWCI*, 51, 184-86.

Kauffmann, C.M. 1966. 'The Bury Bible', *JWCI*, 29, 60-81.

Kendrick, T.D. & Senior, E. 1936. 'St Manchan's Shrine', *Archaeologia*, LXXXVI, 105-18.

Keyser, C.E. 1927. *A List of Norman Tympana and Lintels*. London.

King, D.J.C. *Castellarium Anglicanum*. 2 vols. Millwood, N.Y. & London.

King, J.F. 1990. 'The Old Sarum Master: A Twelfth-Century Sculptor in South-West England', *WANHM*, 83, 70-95.

King, J.F. 1995. 'The Parish Church of Kilpeck Reassessed', *BAA CT*, XV, 82-93.

King, J.F. 1996. 'Sources, Iconography and Context of the Old Sarum Master's Sculpture', *BAA CT*, XVII, 79-84.

Knowles, D. & Hadcock, R.N. 1971. *Medieval Religious Houses in England and Wales*. London.

Krautheimer, R. 1942. 'An Introduction to the Iconography of Medieval Architecture' *JWCI*, 5, 1-33.

Kunstler, G. 1973. *Romanesque Art in Europe*. New York.

Lane, K. 1997. 'Architectural Sculpture in Romanesque England: Forms, Functions and Audience', unpublished Ph.D. thesis, University of East Anglia.

Lees, E. 1879. 'Description of some curious sculptures at Ribbesford Church, Worcestershire', *AASR&P*, XV, 66.

Lewis, C. 1984. 'The Norman Settlement of Herefordshire under William I', *Anglo-Norman Studies*, VII, 195-213.

Lewis, G.R. 1842. *Illustrations of Kilpeck Church, Herefordshire: in a series of drawings made on the spot, with an essay on ecclesiastical design and descriptive interpretation*. London.

Lewis, G.R. 1852. *The Ancient Church of Shobdon, Herefordshire, Illustrated and Described*. London.

Lloyd, J.E. 1912. *A History of Wales from the Earliest Times to the Edwardian Conquest.* 2 vols. London.

Longhurst, M.H. 1927. *Victoria and Albert Museum, Catalogue of Carvings in Ivory*, pt I. London.

Lynam, C. 1905. 'Notes on the Nave of Chepstow Parish Church', *Archaeol. J.,* LXII, 271-78.

Macready, S. & Thompson, F.H. (eds.) 1986. *Art and Patronage in the English Romanesque.* London.

Marshall, G. 1918. 'Remarks on a Norman Tympanum at Fownhope and others in Herefordshire', *TWNFC*, 52-59.

Martin, S.H. 1952-4a. 'St Guthlac, Hereford's forgotten saint', *TWNFC*, 62-69.

Martin, S.H. 1952-4b. 'St Guthlac's Priory and the Citry Churches', *TWNFC*, 219-29.

Martindale, J. 1992. 'Monasteries and Castles: the Priories of St Florent de Saumur in England after 1066, in *England in the Eleventh Century: Harlaxton Medieval Studies*, 2, 135-56.

Megaw, J.V.S. 1970. *Art of the Eurpoean Iron Age.* New York & Evanston.

Meredith, J. 1980. 'The Impact of Italy on the Romanesque Architectural Sculpture of England', unpublished Ph.D. dissertation, Yale University.

Mereweather, J. 1842. *A Statement on the Condition of the Cathedral Church of Hereford.* London.

Morris, R.K. 1983. 'The Herefordshire School: Recent Discoveries', in Thompson 1983, 198-201.

Muratova, X. 1986. 'Bestiaries: an Aspect of Medieval Patronage', in Macready & Thompson, 118-44.

Muratova, X. 1987. 'Les cycles des Bestiaires dans le decor sculpte des églises du XIIe siecle dans le Yorkshire, et leur relation avec les manuscrits des Bestiaires enlumines', *Atti del V Colloquio della International Beast Epic, Fable and Fabliau Society*, Allesandria, 337-54.

Nash-Williams, V.E. 1950. *The Early Christian Monuments of Wales.* Cardiff.

Nichols, S. & Thurlby, M. 1985. 'Notes on the Romanesque Capitals from the East Arch of the Presbytery of Hereford Cathedral', *The Friends of Hereford Cathedral Fifty First Annual Report*, 14-26.

Oliver, G. 1885-6. 'Kilpeck Church, Herefordshire', *AASR&P*, 18, 176-80.

Oman, C. 1958. *The Gloucester Candlestick.* London.

Oursel, R. 1984. *Haut-Poitou Roman.* 2nd edn. La Pierre-qui-Vire (Yonne).

Parker, E; Thurlby, M. & Little, C. 1985. 'Romanesque Re-assembled in England', *Gesta*, XXIV/1, 77-86.

Parker, T.L. 1833. 'Kilpeck Church, Herefordshire', *Gent's Mag.*, CIII/1, 393-95.

Parsons, D. 1995. 'Early Churches in Herefordshire: Documentary and Structural Evidence', *BAA CT*, XV, 60-74.

Patterson, R.B. (ed.) 1973. *Earldom of Gloucester Charters: The Charters and Scribes of the Earls and Countesses of Gloucester to A.D. 1217.* Oxford.

Pettifer, A. 1995. *English Castles: A Guide by Counties.* Woodbridge.

Pevsner, N. 1958. *The Buildings of England, Shropshire.* Harmondsworth.

Pevsner, N. 1963. *The Buildings of England, Herefordshire.* Harmondsworth.

Pevsner, N. 1968. *The Buildings of England, Worcestershire.* Harmondsworth.

Pevsner, N. 1975. *The Buildings of England, Wiltshire.* 2nd edn., revised by B. Cherry, Harmondsworth.

Plant, R. 1994. 'The Cathedral Church of St Mary and St Ethelbert, Hereford: Aspects of its Romanesque Fabric', unpublished M.A. Report, Courtauld Institute of Art, University of London.

Potter, K.R. (ed. & trans.). 1976. *Gesta Stephani*. Oxford.

Prior, E.S. & Gardner, A. 1912. *An Account of Medieval Figure Sculpture in England*. Cambridge.

Radford, C.A.R. 1958. *Goodrich Castle*. London.

Raspi Serra, J. 1969. 'English Decorative Sculpture of the Early Twelfth Century and the Como-Pavian Tradition', *Art Bulletin*, LI, 352-62.

Rees, U. (ed.) 1975. *The Cartulary of Shrewsbury Abbey*, 2 vols. Aberystwyth.

Roberts, E. 1871. 'On Leominster Priory Church', *JBAA*, XXVII, 438-45.

Roberts, G. 1846. 'Llanthony Priory, Monmouthshire', *Arch. Camb.*, I, 210-45.

Rokewode, J.G. 1844. 'Figures of Welsh Knights at Kilpeck', *Archaeologia*, XXX, 62-63.

Roper, J.S. 1978. *A History of St Cassian's Church, Chaddesley Corbett*. Chaddesley Corbett (Worcestershire).

Round, J.H. 1888. *Ancients Charters Royal and Private to A.D. 1200*. London.

Sauerlander, W. 1992. 'Romanesque Sculpture in its Architectural Context', in Kahn 1992a, 17-43.

Schiller, G. 1971. *Iconography of Christian Art*, Vol. 1. New York.

Scott, Sir G.G. 1877. 'Hereford Cathedral', *Archaeol. J.*, LVIII, 323-48.

Shoesmith, R. 1983. 'St Guthlac's Priory, Hereford', *TWNFC*, XLIV, pt 3, 321-57.

Shoesmith R. 1991. 'Excavations at Chepstow 1973-4', *Cambrian Archaeology* Monograpgh No.4

Shoesmith, R. 1992. 'Excavations at Kilpeck, Herefordshire', *TWNFC*, XLVII, pt 2, 162-209.

Smith, J.T. 1963. 'The Norman Structure of Leominster Priory Church', *Transactions of the Ancient Monuments Society*, N.S. II, 97-108.

Speake, G. 1980. *Anglo-Saxon Animal Art and its Germanic Background*. Oxford.

Stalley, R.A. 'A 12th-Century Patron of Architecture: A study of the buildings erected by Roger, Bishop of Salisbury', *JBAA*, 3rd ser., 34, 62-83.

Stalley, R.A. 1981. 'Three Irish Buildings with West Country Origins', *BAA CT*, IV 62-80.

Stalley R.A. 1996. *Irish High Crosses*. Dublin.

Stoker, C.H. 1908-11. 'Brinsop Church', *TWNFC*, 163-66.

Stone, L. 1955. *Sculpture in Britain: The Middle Ages*. Harmondsworth.

Strong, Dr. 1849. 'Fownhope Church, Herefordshire', *The Builder*, VII, 80.

Swynnerton, C. 1921. 'The Priory Church of St Leonard at Stanley, Co. Gloucester, in the light of recent discoveries documentary and structural', *Archaeologia*, 71, 199-226.

Taylor, A.J. 1951. *Monmouth Castle and Great Castle House*. London.

Taylor, H.M. 1978. *Anglo-Saxon Architecture*. III. Cambridge.

Taylor, H.M. & Taylor, J. 1965. *Anglo-Saxon Architecture*. 2 vols. Cambridge.

Tchericover, A. 1989. 'Romanesque Sculpted Archivolts in Western France. Forms and Techniques', *Arte Medievale*, 2nd ser., Anno 3, no. 1, 49-75.

Temple, E. 1976. *Anglo-Saxon Manuscripts 900-1066*. London.

Thompson, F.H. (ed.) 1983. *Studies in Medieval Sculpture*. London.

Thompson, M.W. 1986. 'Associated Monasteries and Castles in the Middle Ages: A Tentative List', *Archaeol. J.* 143, 305-21.

Thurlby, M. 1980. 'Romanesque Sculpture at Tewkesbury Abbey', *TBGAS*, XCVIII, 89-94.

Thurlby, M. 1982a. 'Fluted and Chalice-Shaped: The Aylesbury Group of Fonts', *Country Life* (January 28), 228-29.

Thurlby, M. 1982b. 'A Note on the Twelfth-Century Sculpture from Old Sarum Cathedral', *WANHM*, 76, 93-98.

Thurlby, M. 1984. 'A note on the romanesque sculpture at Hereford Cathedral and the Herefordshire School of Sculpture', *Burl. Mag.*, CXXVI, no. 973, 233-34.

Thurlby, M. 1985. 'The Elevations of the Romanesque Abbey Churches of St Mary at Tewkesbury and St Peter at Gloucester', **BAA CT**, VII, 36-51.
Thurlby, M. 1988a. 'The Former Romanesque High Vault in the Presbytery of Hereford Cathedral', *JSAH*, XLVII, 185-89.
Thurlby, M. 1988b. 'The Romanesque Priory Church of St Michael at Ewenny', *JSAH*, XLVII, 281-94.
Thurlby, M. 1991. 'The Romanesque Cathedral of St Mary and St Peter at Exeter', *BAA CT*, XI, 19-34.
Thurlby, M. 1994a. 'The Roles of the Patron and the Master Mason in the First Design of the Romanesque Cathedral of Durham', in *Anglo-Norman Durham 1093-1193*, ed. D. Rollason *et al*, Woodbridge, 161-84.
Thurlby, 1994b. 'The Romanesque Apse Vault at Peterborough Cathedral', in Buckton & Heslop, 171-86.
Thurlby, M. 1995a. 'Hereford Cathedral: The Romanesque Fabric', *BAA CT*, XV, 15-28.
Thurlby, 1995b. 'The Lady Chapel of Glastonbury Abbey', *Antiq. J.*, 75, 107-70.
Thurlby, M. 1995c. 'Jedburgh AbBey church: the Romanesque fabric', *Proceedings of the Society of Antiquaries of Scotland*, 125, 793-812.
Thurlby, M. 1996. 'The Abbey Church, Pershore: An Architectural History', *Transactions of the Worcestershire Archaeological Society*, 3rd ser., 15, 146-209.
Thurlby, M. 1997, 'L'abbatiale romane de St Albans', in Bayle 1997, 79-90.
Thurlby, M. & Kusaba, Y. 1991. 'The Nave of Saint Andrew at Steyning: A Study of Variety in Design in Twelfth-Century Architecture in Britain', *Gesta*, XXX/2, 163-75.
Tonkin, J.W. 1982-84. 'Herefordshire Castles', *TWNFC*, 44, 31-35.
Toynbee, J.M.C. 1962. *Art in Roman Britain*. London.
Toynbee, J.M.C. 1964. *Art in Britain under the Romans*. London.
Toynbee, J.M.C. & Ward Perkins, J. 1956. *The Shrine of St Peter*. London.
Ulansey, D. 1989. *The Origins of the Mithraic Mysteries*. Oxford.
Vermaseen, M.J. 1963. *Mithras: The Secret God*. London.
VCH Gloucestershire, II (1907).
VCH Gloucestershire, VIII (1968).
VCH Gloucestershire, X (1972).
VCH Herefordshire, I (1908).
VCH Shropshire, I (1908).
VCH Shropshire, II (1973).
VCH Warwickshire, I (1904).
VCH Worcestershire, III (1913).
VCH Worcestershire, IV (1924).
Walker, D. 1958. 'Miles of Gloucester, Earl of Hereford', *TBGAS*, LXXVII, 66-84.
Walker, D. 1960. 'The "Honours" of the Earls of Hereford in the Twelfth Century', *TBGAS*, LXXIX, 174-211.
Walker, D. 1964. 'Charters of the Earldom of Hereford 1095-1201', Camden Miscellany, 22, 4th ser., I, 1-76.
Walker, D. 1969. 'William Fitz Osbern and the Norman Settlement in Herefordshire',*TWNFC*, XXXIX, 402-12.
Walker, D. 1974. 'Brecon Priory in the Middle Ages', in *Links with the Past: Swansea and Brecon Historical Essays*, ed. O.W. Jones & D. Walker. Llandybie, Carmarthenshire, 37-65.
Walker, D. 1976. 'A Register of the Churches of the Monastery of St Peter's Gloucester', *An Ecclesiastical Miscellany, Bristol and Gloucestershire Archaeological Society*, XI, 3-49.

Wathen, J. 1789. 'Description of Kilpec Church in Herefordshire', *Gent's Mag.*, LIX, 781.

Watkins, M.G. 1905-7. 'Rowlstone Church', *TWNFC*, 264-68.

Webster, J.C. 1938. *The Labors of the Month in Antique and Medieval Art*. Evanston and Chicago.

Weir, A. & Jerman, J. 1986. *Images of Lust: Sexual Carvings on Medieval Churches*. London.

Welander, D. 1991. *The History, Art and Architecture of Gloucester Cathedral*. Stroud.

West, J.K. 1988. 'Architectural Sculpture in the Parish Churches of the 11th- and 12th-Century West Midlands: Some Problems in Assessing the Evidence', in Blair 1988a, 159-68.

Wharton, H. 1691. *Anglia Sacra*. 2 vols.

White, T.H. 1960. *The Bestiary: A Book of Beasts*. New York.

Whtehead, D. 1995. 'The Mid-Nineteenth-Century Restoration of Hereford Cathedral by Lewis Knockalls Cottingham, 1842-1850', *BAA CT*, XV, 176-86.

Whitfield, N. 1993. 'The Filigree of the Hunterston and "Tara" Brooches', in *The Art of Migrating Ideas*, ed. R.M. Spearman, Edinburgh.

Wightman, W.E. 1966. *The Lacy Family in England and Normandy 1066-1194*. Oxford.

Williamson, P. 1982. *An Introduction to Medieval Ivory Carvings*. London.

Williamson, P. *Catalogue of Romanesque Sculpture: Victoria and Albert Museum*. London.

Williamson, P. 1995. *Gothic Sculpture 1130-1300*. New Haven and London.

Willis, R. 1842. *Report of a Survey of the Dilapidated Portions of Hereford Cathedral in the Year 1841*. Hereford. Reprinted in *Architectural History of some English Cathedrals*, II. Chicheley, 1973.

Wood, I. 1985. 'Areas of Tension 900-1200', *Art History*, VIII, 228-34.

Wright, T. 1845. 'The Remains of Shobdon Church', *Archaeol. J.*, I, 233-37.

Zarnecki, G. 1951a. *English Romanesque Sculpture 1066-1140*. London.

Zarnecki, G. 1953. *Later English Romanesque Sculpture 1140-1210*. London.

Zarnecki, G. 1978. 'The Romaneque Capitals in the South Transept of Worcester Cathedral', *BAA CT*, I, 38-42.

Zarnecki, G. 1979. *Studies in Romanesque Sculpture*. London.

Zarnecki, G. 1986. 'Sculpture in Stone in the English Romanesque Art Exhibition', in Macready and Thompson, 7-27.

Zarnecki,G. 1988. *Romanesque Lincoln: The Sculpture of the Cathedral*. Lincoln

Zarnecki, G. 1990. 'Germanic Animal Motifs in Romanesque Sculpture', *Artibus et Historiae*, 22(XI), 189-203.

Zarnecki, G. 1991. 'Corpus of Romanesque Sculpture in Britain and Ireland', *Kunstchronik*, 44, 611-13.

Zarnecki, G. 1992. *Further Studies in Romanesque Sculpture*. London.

Zarnecki, G. 1993. 'The Future of the Shobdon Arches', *JBAA*, CXLVI, 87-92.

Zarnecki, G. 1994. 'The Priory Church of Shobdon and its Founder', in Buckton & Heslop, 211-20.

Zarnecki, G. 1997. 'La sculpture romane des "Marches Gauloises"', in Bayle 1997, 91-109.

Zarnecki, G.; Holt, J. & Holland, T., (eds.) 1984. *English Romanesque Art 1066-1200*, Exhibition Catalogue, Hayward Gallery, London.

Zarnecki, J. [G.]. 1951b. 'Regional Schools of English Sculpture in the Twelfth Century', unpublished Ph.D. thesis, University of London.

INDEX